SANCTIFIED BY
GOD

SANCTIFIED BY GOD

A Call to Keep the Christian Sabbath

By Daniel E. Horn

with Joshua E. Horn

Reforming To Scripture Press
www.ReformingToScripture.com

Second Edition: Novenber 2010
First Edition: December 2009

Reforming To Scripture Press
8229 Zebulon Road
Youngsville, North Carolina 27596
www.ReformingToScripture.com

ISBN-13: 978-0-9843696-1-4
ISBN-10: 0-9843696-1-9

Cover Photo by Joshua Horn
Cover Design by Nic Ruiz
Book Layout by Joshua Horn

Printed in the United States of America

All scripture quotes Authorized (King James) Version.

MORE BOOKS
from Reforming to Scripture

Communion of Christ's Body

In the New Testament, we are given two sacraments to picture the gospel: baptism and the Lord's Supper. God has given us the Lord's Supper to be a clear picture of the cost to Jesus Christ for our salvation as well as a promise of future blessing. When we properly partake of Communion in faith, God uses it to cleanse us and sanctify us. The desire of the authors of this book is that the church reforms its practice of the Lord's Supper so that the Lord's death is properly proclaimed until He comes.

From Glory to Glory

Importance of Old Testament Law to
New Testament Believers

(Avaliable 2011)

Santificado Por Dio

Dios nos manda "Sed santos, porque yo soy santo." La primera vez que Dios declara algo santo, no es acerca de una persona, sino de un día. Por apartar ese día, Él estableció un patrón a seguir para todo hombre en todo lugar y los que no lo sigan están rebelándose contra Dios. Estamos para guardar el Día de Reposo santo como señal de que Dios nos ha apartado para Él Mismo. Este libro es un llamado para Cristianos a regresar a guardar El Día de Reposo y a caminar como un pueblo santificado por Dios.

(Disponibles 2011)

Available Online at

www.ReformingToScripture.com

Table of Contents

Preface

This book originated from a sermon series given at Hope Baptist Church in Wake Forest, North Carolina, during May and June of 2009 where I am an elder. In considering the shepherding that was needed for that church, the elders started to consider what behavior was going on after Sunday services after preaching on the fourth commandment. At our church, the time the congregants sit together during the Sunday morning worship service is not their only time of interaction. As a church, we have been focused on reforming our practices to those that are found in scripture. God has told us in scripture how we are to worship Him and our responsibility is to conform to it to the best of our understanding. Because the pattern in the early church appears to be the sharing of an agape meal every Lord's Day, that is our practice as well. It is typical on a Sunday for most of the people that came for the worship service that started at ten in the morning to fellowship until two or three in the afternoon. Because we were able to observe our congregation as it interacts on the Sabbath, it made us ask ourselves the question: were our practices on Sunday afternoon biblical, or were we doing our own pleasure?

Preaching through a series of five sermons on the Sabbath and exhorting the congregation to biblical practices, we saw the members go through a series of reactions. The first reaction was one of considering that we were becoming legalistic. How could the elders say that God has told us how we are to spend our time on the Sabbath? How can the elders say that we are not to buy and sell on the Sabbath? That position is constraining our freedom in Christ. But as we brought the scriptures to bear on the issue, more people became almost angry. But then the merciful God started to bring conviction to the congregation and people began to realize that they were pursuing their own pleasures rather than the will of God. As the sermon series ended, we saw the people begin to reform their practices. It is truly a blessing of God to see Him bring conviction and repentance to His people.

That is the background that drives the writing of this book. Our desire is that the church in America taste some of the blessings that we have received; a greater joy in being together and a better witness to those around us. May God give us each ears to hear the wondrous things that are in His law.

Daniel E. Horn
November 28th, 2009

P.S. - If after you have read the book, you still have arguments as to why the Sabbath is abrogated, please send us a note. We may not be able to answer you, but we will consider your comments for the next edition.

You can e-mail any questions or comments to:

SanctifiedByGod@ReformingToScripture.com

CHAPTER 1

The Question

Too often, when talking about the applicability of the Sabbath, the discussion starts in the wrong place. Typically, we start with the thought, "How can I get out of doing this?" Instead, we should be asking, "Does God really call me to such a wonderful thing?" To understand the importance of the difference, consider this scenario. A husband asks his wife to spend the day with him. If she said, "Do I really have to?" or, "You are so demanding," we would not consider her a good wife. A good wife should desire to spend time with her husband. Now perhaps her attitude is antagonized by poor qualities in her husband, but fundamentally the fact that she does not desire to be with her husband is a bad sign for their marriage. Or consider the wife whose response to the request from her husband is, "I will give you a couple of hours in the morning." Anyone looking at this situation would not admire the wife for her dedication to the marriage. They would say the wife is trying to negotiate down her obligations as much as possible and not desiring to strengthen or support the marriage. Instead of that scenario, suppose that she said, "That would be great as long as we can get this shopping done and do the laundry. I would love to spend the day with you, as long as we can meet my agenda. But for a couple hours in the morning, we will do whatever you want." We would consider her to be a better wife, but she could hardly be called a helpmeet for her husband, since her agenda is taking precedent. She is trying to rule the household. Again, this is not the sign of a good wife or a good marriage.

A Good Wife

If we are trying to describe what a good wife should do in that scenario, we would say she should first start with a desire to spend the day with her husband. Her desire should be to spend that day with the love of her life, and she should delight in spending that time with him. A good wife would try to reschedule everything that she can, so that she can have that time with him without any distractions. She should desire more of that time because it is good for their relationship. She would try to get everything done that she can beforehand, so there is less chance of interruption during that time with him. A good wife would desire to spend that time in the way that her husband declares the most profitable, if he is a faithful husband desiring what is best for her.

In the end, the purpose of this book is to advocate that the church, the bride of Christ, is to be a faithful wife to her husband. If we start with the question, "Would God really tell us we have to keep the Sabbath?" we are starting with an attitude that we do not want to spend time with our husband. That is the sad state of affairs throughout most of the church in the twenty-first century. We are a bad wife who is trying to figure out any excuse not to keep the Sabbath. We are starting not with an attitude of love toward God, but with an attitude that while we want Him to save us from eternal damnation, that is the only use we have for Him. Instead, our complete desire is to be for Him because, "in Him we live and move and have our being."[1] When we are looking for an excuse to not devote ourselves to Him, to restrict the time that we spend with Him, or to set our own agenda for that time rather than accepting His, we are rejecting a wonderful gift that God is giving us. Instead our attitude should be, "Has God really asked us to do that?"

Consider the fact that we are but dust that God breathed into and gave life, then He died on the cross so that we can live eternally with Him. These things are to be marvelous in our eyes. These are things that are not understandable to us because He is infinite, almighty and pure, and we are finite, weak and defiled. So if He is calling us to spend the day with Him, we should truly delight in that. We should marvel in that. We should desire to be a good wife to that husband who we are not at all deserving of. Do you understand what an insult it is to God to say, "Do we really have to? Must we spend time with Him? We have more things of this world that we want to pursue." Or even, "We are working to establish the kingdom of God by our own strength, and we need to pursue that instead of spending time with God." That is building with wood, hay and stubble, instead of gold and silver. We need to be a bride that submits to her husband and desires to do the will of her husband, instead of what is right in her own eyes.

---

1. Acts 17:28a.

3

Which Is Your Question?

Now it is crucial to study the Scriptures to see what it says on this matter, but your interpretation is dependent upon your attitude as you approach those Scriptures. It is important to ask yourself, "What answer am I hoping for? Do I want Christ to be declaring that He wants to spend time with me, or do I just want to be 'free in Christ' to do whatever I want?" In the type that God gave us between Christ and His church, i.e. marriage, we understand that there appears to be a loss of certain aspects of freedom so that greater things can be gained. Why would we think that the antetype would be any different? When we become betrothed to Christ, we receive wonderful benefits, but now we need to consider our husband, while before we ignored Him. In other words, the question that each of us needs to ask ourselves as we approach the Sabbath is not, "How can I get out of doing this?" but, "Oh God, did you really call me to such a wonderful thing?" "Do You, the Lord of Lords and King of Kings really desire to spend time with me?" We should rejoice that the husband of the church is a good and loving master who only only wants what is best for his bride. The question to ask yourself as you read this book is, do you trust that what God wants for you is better for you than what you want for yourself?

4

CHAPTER 2

The Need

O ur goal in writing this book is for the church to return to a view that we are to delight in God by keeping His Sabbath because of its testimony to the world that
God is a cleansing fire, that God is active and sovereign over
all things today. The Bible is not a dead history book, but a
living book that defines how we are to live. The sovereign
God who brought forth the events that are recorded in its
pages is the same God who brings forth the events that are
reported in today's media. But we need to be doing more
than declare that the Sabbath must be kept, because many
people believe that they are keeping the Sabbath. They go
to church on Sunday, and spend two or three hours with the
people of God listening to teaching and preaching. Then after they have "kept" the Sabbath, everyone is eager to get out
of church so they do not miss kickoff. How far have we come
as a nation from the early 1930s, when it was illegal in some
states to play football on Sunday[1], to the present day where
church services are shortened to make certain that people

---

1. New York Times, November 12 1933, *First Legal Sabbath Contest Since 1794
    To Be Held on Philadelphia Field Sunday* http://select.nytimes.com/gst/ab-
    stract.html?res=F00E15F83C5516738DDDA80994D9415B838FF1D3,   Ac-
    cessed November 25 2009.

arrive home in time for the game or the churches them-selves host Superbowl parties. This book is also an attempt to call us back to keeping a biblical Sabbath and not the wa-tered-down Sabbath that is typically kept today. To keep the Sabbath is not just to go to church, rather it is to turn your foot from your own pleasures and focus on worshiping God for a twenty-four hour day.

Rather than delighting in its God, the church today sees the time that it is to spend with Him as an obligation instead of a delight. The people of Jesus Christ were lost sinners that He took out of the world, and cleansed them and made them sons and daughters. We should marvel that God was so mer-ciful and gracious to us, that He does more than just save us from our sins, but saves us to become children of the living God. The Sabbath is about gathering as a spiritual family and spending the day with our Father. Since Jesus Christ is the husband of the church, it is also a day for us to spend with our husband. The church in America today considers it slavery to spend time with its husband. Our desire is for this book to declare the wonderful things that God has for His children, so that we recognize that His ways are far bet-ter than our ways, and that the Sabbath is a wonderful gift to man.

Freedom in Christ

A call to keep the Christian Sabbath seems to be very out of place in our day and age. The church today focuses on what they call the freedom that is in Christ. Everyone who has been saved by His blood understands the importance of being saved from the curse of the Law and everlasting punishment in hell. It is good and proper that we celebrate that freedom from the curse, but when we take it and pervert it into "we can do whatever we want," it is a different gospel than that preached by Christ and the Apostles. Jesus said:

Ye are my friends, if ye do whatsoever I command you.[2]

When we look to a freedom that is something other than freedom from the enslavement of sin and want freedom from the call of Christ to do those things that He commanded us, we have actually rejected Him as Lord in our lives even as we profess Him with our tongues. Instead, we need to be celebrating that we have been made slaves of righteousness.

Every man who has ever been born, except Jesus Christ, has started out worshiping himself. He thinks that when he commands, the world should obey. As he grows and becomes a man, he continues as a slave to the flesh, because the natural man can only know things of the flesh. Then Jesus Christ effectually calls him and sets him free. But the freedom that he is given is different than the church is proclaiming today.

Then said Jesus to those Jews which believed on him, If ye continue in my word, then are ye my disciples indeed; And ye shall know the truth, and the truth shall make you free.[3]

The freedom that Christ gives in salvation is not freedom from the law, it is freedom from the curse and condemnation of the law. Christians should still desire to keep the law, because that is how our Father reveals his righteousness to us.

---

2. John 15:14.
3. John 8:31-32.

The Inerrancy of Scripture

In many ways, we do live in a very hopeful age. Over the last thirty years, two movements of God have arisen in the church that promise better things to come. The first movement is a revival of the doctrine of the inerrancy of scripture. After many years of this doctrine being under attack, many people began to recognize once again that if we can act as editors of scripture and pick and choose which parts of the Bible we want to keep, we are making a god in our image instead of seeking the true God who created us in His image. The result of the doctrine of the inerrancy of scripture is that we have the ability to know God's will, because He has written an unchangeable book in which we can discover it. This doctrine has caused a renewal of a focus on expository preaching and God's people learning more about the full council of God rather than just the the areas of passion of the preacher.

The Doctrines of Grace

Following the enlightenment of the importance of God's word has been the second movement - a rediscovery within many denominations of the doctrines of grace. By a correct understanding of how we come into relationship with a triune God, we have a picture of the God who is described in scripture. The God who does all things for His glory. The God who is truly transcendent over all things, so the church again is beginning to understand how David can cry out that he is just dust.[4] The God who created all things, and continues to direct them by His own will without considering

---

4.   Psalm 103:14 "For he knoweth our frame; he remembereth that we are dust."

our counsel. The effect across denominations of the church has been a revival of reverence toward God and a delight in knowing this God who is perfect and holy and not dependent on us in any way. When we truly understand that we are creatures who deserve God's eternal wrath, but in its place receive the incredible blessing of being adopted as sons, our correct response is worship.

Not a Grievous Command

So why a book on the Sabbath? Because the Sabbath is one of the biblical signs of true worship. It is not a sign because we gather as a church, fellowship together, sing songs, hear the preaching of the word, and take the Lord's Supper. All of those things are an important part of the worship on the Lord's day, but in this book the concern is not in those things, but in the actual keeping of the Sabbath by turning from our work and desiring to rest in God. God says in 1 John:

> For this is the love of God, that we keep his commandments: and his commandments are not grievous.[5]

God gives all commands for two reasons: for His own eternal glory, and for the good of those who love God and are the called according to His purpose.[6] These two reasons are not contradictory, but rather complementary. When we read His commandments, such as to keep the Sabbath holy, our response needs to be that this commandment is not grievous, because God gives all commands for our good.

---

5   1 John 5:3.
6.   Romans 8:28 " And we know that all things work together for good to them that love God, to them who are the called according to his purpose."

Whether the command was given in the Old Testament or New Testament era, God has never given any grievous commandments. According to our feeble understanding, obeying the command might make things worse for us. It might make us lose money or detract from our pleasure, but God knows more than us and we need to accept that His commands are correct in every situation. When we recognize the grace of God, our response needs to be to examine His commandments and to take delight in our obedience to them. 1 Timothy says:

> *Furthermore then we beseech you, brethren, and exhort you by the Lord Jesus, that as ye have received of us how ye ought to walk and to please God, so ye would abound more and more.*[7]

As the church rediscovers lost doctrines, we can respond in two ways. We could be satisfied with where we are and be puffed up in all the many things we know about God, or we can grow in sanctification and apply those doctrines to our lives.

Sanctified From the World

We are not set apart from the world by our knowledge. We are set apart from the world because we are saved by God from our sins and have had our hearts circumcised by the Holy Spirit which is shown by our love, both our love for God and for our neighbor. As God sanctifies us, He conforms us to His image and convicts and chastises us so that we obey His commandments. From Ezekiel 20:12:

---

7 1 Timothy 4:1.

10

Moreover also I gave them my sabbaths, to be a sign between me and them, that they might know that I am the LORD that sanctify them.

One of the purposes of the Sabbath is to testify that it is God who sanctifies us and not our work. When we do not keep the Sabbath holy, what we are testifying is either that we are not sanctified, or that sanctification is the work of man. Keeping the Sabbath shows that salvation is a real thing, because when you are saved, God changes you so that you obey His commands.

Judgment for Disobedience

The desire in writing this book is to raise an awareness of how seriously God considers the keeping of the Sabbath. God sent Judah into captivity because they refused to keep the Sabbath. Nehemiah said this to the people of Israel, rebuking them for breaking the Sabbath:

Did not your fathers thus, and did not our God bring all this evil upon us, and upon this city? yet ye bring more wrath upon Israel by profaning the sabbath.[8]

If we desire for God to remove the curse from our nation, as Christians we must humble ourselves before God, repent and rejoice in the day that God has set aside for our good.

Structure of the Book

This book is split into two parts. The next four chapters are an argument for why we should continue to keep the Sabbath today. First, the commandment will be considered so that we understand just how important the Sabbath has

---

8. Nehemiah 13:18.

always been as a testimony to the world of who God is and what He does. The next chapter is a rebuttal to those who say that the Sabbath was abrogated, that it is a ceremonial law that does not apply today. It is sad that we would desire not to receive this gift from God which we have in the Sabbath. But since many argue that it no longer applies to God's people, those arguments are addressed. The rest of this section of the book expresses how God has punished His people for violating the Sabbath as a warning to us. There is also a chapter describing that the position of this book is the historical position of the church, and that the church in America is ignoring the testimonies of our fathers in the faith.

The next section of the book is to clarify what scripture says about the practice of keeping the Sabbath. When the Pharisees first decided to kill Jesus, it was because He healed on the Sabbath.

And therefore did the Jews persecute Jesus, and sought to slay him, because he had done these things on the sabbath day. [9]

When Jesus Christ healed on the Sabbath, the Pharisees determined to kill Him, because in their mind, He was violating the Sabbath. They considered that He was worthy of death because of what He did on the Sabbath day. Once we agree that the Sabbath needs to be kept, then we need to study the word of God, so that we do not follow the path of the Pharisees and create rules where God did not. By doing so, we can turn what God gave to be a blessing into a curse. Our aim in that section is to present some of the principles that

---

9.   John 5:16.

should be considered when meditating on what things are proper and not proper to do on God's holy day.

CHAPTER 3

The Sanctification

The argument for why Christians today are commanded
to keep the Sabbath starts with an understanding of
what the commandment has always been about. The fourth
commandment is about holiness. It is about being set apart.
It is about not being of this world while remaining in this
world as a testimony to the grace and mercy of God.

> *But as he which hath called you is holy, so be ye holy in
> all manner of conversation; Because it is written, Be ye
> holy; for I am holy.*[1]

God commands us to be a special people that He has called
to Himself. We are to be a people that are different in all of
our ways, because God will make it so. When we are saved,
God changes us from doing what is right in our own eyes
to desiring to do what is right in His eyes by His sovereign
choice.

The fourth commandment is about God proclaim-
ing that He is sovereign over every aspect of this world and
that He specifically wants to make that be proclaimed to the
world by how His people use their time. When the people

---

1.   1 Peter 1:15-16.

who profess Christ are still focused on themselves, they are acting as a people who still do not know the truth.

For of him, and through him, and to him, are all things: to whom be glory for ever. Amen.[2]

The purpose of the world is to bring glory to God. As His people, we need to understand that just as the Sabbath in the Old Testament was to proclaim that God's people are set apart to Him, God's people in the New Testament are equally set apart to Him. That those who have put their faith in Jesus Christ continue to have the responsibility to proclaim that we are not like the rest of the world. When God gave us the ten commandments on Mount Sinai, He was declaring in stone the moral duty of all men which was written in the flesh of Adam's heart before the fall. That moral duty continues to apply to us today and by studying the commandment, we need to understand why the fourth commandment in particular still applies today.

Three-fold Sanctification

As we consider the Sabbath, we need to understand that the Sabbath is about sanctification in three ways. It is about first how God has sanctified us to himself, how God is sanctified from this world, and lastly how God is the one that is sanctifying us. To understand how God sets us apart by the Sabbath, we need to consider the words of the commandment in Exodus 20:8-11:

Remember the Sabbath day, to keep it holy. Six days you shall labor and do all your work, but the seventh

---

2.   Romans 11:36.

day is the Sabbath of the LORD your God. In it you shall do no work: you, nor your son, nor your daughter, nor your male servant, nor your female servant, nor your cattle, nor your stranger who is within your gates. For in six days the LORD made the heavens and the earth, the sea, and all that is in them, and rested the seventh day. Therefore the LORD blessed the Sabbath day and hallowed it.

The heart of the fourth commandment is not about whether we work or not. The commandment starts with the idea that the Sabbath day must be holy. The day is holy and is to be kept holy. It is to be separated from the rest of the week, and that is the heart of the commandment. We keep the day holy partly by not working like the other six days, but the main focus of the commandment is not us keeping the day holy, but that the day is holy unto the Lord. In this giving of the commandment, we can understand that it is God who sanctified the Sabbath, not man.

The Sabbath Sanctified in Creation

The creation week started with six days in which God worked. He created the heavens and the earth and all of the things therein. On the sixth day, He created man and woman and He gave them work to do:

And God blessed them, and God said unto them, Be fruitful, and multiply, and replenish the earth, and subdue it: and have dominion over the fish of the sea, and over the fowl of the air, and over every living thing that moveth upon the earth.[3]

3.   Genesis 1:28.

17

God gave us that work to do as a blessing. We might have a tendency to consider that the days that God has given us to work are a curse, but God has stated very specifically that the assignment of work was a blessing from the mouth of God. When we think instead that we will be better off if we chase our own pleasures, we need to understand true joy is through obedience to God and by obeying His command for us to work. But even with those joys that are to come from doing the work that our Father has commanded us, there were still greater joys that God gave us.

> *And on the seventh day God ended his work which he had made; and he rested on the seventh day from all his work which he had made. And God blessed the seventh day, and sanctified it: because that in it he had rested from all his work which God created and made.*[4]

God blessed the seventh day and sanctified it and, because He had rested on it, we get to partake of that rest on a weekly basis. When Christians say that they are not bound by the Sabbath, what they are saying is that a day that God separated from the rest, that God blessed, is not a blessing but a curse. Let God be true and every man a liar![5] When we say that the Sabbath day is a burden that God is forcing us to bear, we are contradicting the clear words of scripture, that this day is holy and blessed.

Responsibility to Sanctify

The Sabbath is not just to be sanctified by how the

---

4. Genesis 2:2-3.
5. Romans 3:4 " God forbid: yea, let God be true, but every man a liar; as it is written, That thou mightest be justified in thy sayings, and mightest overcome when thou art judged."

righteous are blessed through rest on that day; the righteous are to testify to its being holy by how they treat others. You are to exercise the authority you have been given to sanctify the day. The father and mother have authority over their sons and daughters. They have the responsibility to testify to the existence of God through how they treat their children. By keeping the Sabbath, we teach our children to know who God is, that He is holy and separate from the world. When we do not keep the Sabbath, we testify that it is our strength that preserves us and not the work of God's hand. We testify to them that we have not been set apart to God, irrespective of whether we say we have been. Our actions will always speak louder than our words, especially to our children. When we work on the Sabbath even though God told us not to, we testify that we do not trust that if we obey His commands He will provide. Instead, we prove that we really think we need to provide by our own strength. We pray, "Give us this day our daily bread,"[6] and we give thanks for what God does, but then we turn around and play the hypocrite by working to provide for ourselves the bread, contrary to how God said we were to receive it.

Consider how different the testimony is to your children if you keep the Sabbath instead of ignoring it. Clearly, from scripture, there is a responsibility to be declaring who the sovereign God is to your children everyday.[7] But even with that testimony proclaiming who God is as you live your daily life, consider the impact of a weekly testifying that God is the

---

6. Matthew 6:11.
7. Deuteronomy 6:7 " And thou shalt teach them diligently unto thy children, and shalt talk of them when thou sittest in thine house, and when thou walkest by the way, and when thou liest down, and when thou risest up."

Provider, that God is the one to whom you owe service every minute of the day, and that God is a loving Father. If we are doing the work that God has given us to do and are involving our children in that as we should, then the pattern of a day of rest in our life is saying that our Father in heaven loves us and has blessed us with a day every week to rest and delight in our God. If the child lives at home until eighteen years old, that is almost a thousand days that we have a focused testimony of the love of God. When we fail to keep the Sabbath, we rob our children of this testimony that God commanded should be before their eyes.

But the command does not end there. God has required us to testify to those over whom we have authority of the sanctity of the day by letting them rest. All of your man servants and maid servants are to get a day of rest. It is easy for us in this day and age to say we do not have servants so this does not apply, but restaurants boom on the Lord's Day. Those people in the restaurants and stores that we pay to fill our needs are our servants. They are not in lengthy service to us as they have been in previous ages, such as when slavery was practiced, but they are still serving us. When we pay people to provide services to us on the Sabbath, we are testifying to them that we do not believe that it is God who provides even for the unjust. We are testifying that man is ultimately the one that provides for them. We are saying to look toward man for your daily bread. When we do business on the Sabbath, we are sinning against those servers, because we are removing the testimony of the Sabbath that God has commanded for the unbeliever. Additionally, we take away their opportunity to attend church on the Lord's Day, so they can hear the testimony of God.

Kindness to Animals

The command goes on to include giving even your cattle the day of rest. Do we see how we have perverted the word of God, when we say that this does not continue in the New Testament era? If the Sabbath indeed ended in the New Testament era, then in the Old Testament, the Israelites were required to let even their oxen rest, but Jesus changed all of that. Now, as Christians, we have no responsibility to give our cattle rest. We can make them work seven days, because Jesus Christ shed His blood for us. Is this the picture of love that we are supposed to be? When God threatened to destroy Nineveh, He rebuked Jonah for not being concerned about the people in the city, because Jonah was more concerned about his comfort. In God's rebuke, He asked Jonah:

> *And should not I spare Nineveh, that great city, wherein are more than sixscore thousand persons that cannot discern between their right hand and their left hand; and also much cattle?* [8]

God has always cared about His creation. Proverbs 12:10 says:

> *A righteous man regardeth the life of his beast: but the tender mercies of the wicked are cruel.*

Just as the righteous man in the Old Testament was to show mercy to his animals, we are not free to be cruel because we have been freed in Christ. We have been freed to become

---

8. Jonah 4:11.

a slave of righteousness, so we have a greater obligation to honor the Sabbath with how we treat our animals. But we should not take this to false conclusions. For instance, we could say we should not drive our cars on the Sabbath because we should give them rest. But they are not living. God clearly distinguishes between those things which are living and those which are not. None of the commandments are to protect inanimate objects, because they do not need rest.

Definition of Work

There is a commandment not to "kindle a fire on the Sabbath day,"[9] but this is not to give the fire rest. This commandment shows what it means for men to rest. Those things that can be done before the Sabbath should be done before. The gathering of fire wood should be done before the Sabbath day and the fire started. It does not mean that wood cannot be added to a fire that is already burning. Later, we will discuss what constitutes unlawful work on the Sabbath.[10]

The Pharisees perverted the law of God from being a kindness to being a yoke impossible to bear. Those things that can be done on the Day of Preparation should be done before the Sabbath, but God continued to work even on the last day of creation week which we know because Jesus said:

> *And therefore did the Jews persecute Jesus, and sought to slay him, because he had done these things on the sabbath day. But Jesus answered them, My Father worketh hitherto, and I work.*[11]

---

9. Exodus 35:3 "Ye shall kindle no fire throughout your habitations upon the sabbath day."
10. Chapter 7, *The Rest*.
11. John 5:16-17.

22

Christ is making the argument that what the Jews were call-ing work must be acceptable to happen on the Sabbath, be-cause if God adopted their stringent definition, then He was not resting on the seventh day as He said in His word. When we consider what is the correct biblical definition of work, we need to be certain that our definition does not make Jesus Christ a sinner, because we know that there was no fault in Him.[12]

Responsibility of the State

The last group that the commandment states must be given rest is the foreigner. Biblically, the foreigner is someone who is not part of the people of God. This does not include those who are part of a Christian household. The Sabbath is also a commandment to the society.

God commands different jurisdictions to enforce this command. Fathers are to command their sons and daughters to keep the Sabbath holy, but they are not the only ones who have responsibility. The nation is judged for its failure to keep the Sabbath. The foreigner referred to in the commandment is a person who is not within the jurisdiction of an Israelite family nor of the Levitical priesthood. A foreigner within the gates of your city would not keep the Sabbath on his own, so it is clear that it should be enforced by the state.

The idea that the state should enforce laws related to the first table of the law in our day and age is rejected. In America, the church claims to hold to a biblical definition of the separation of church and state. The true biblical doc-trine of the separation of church and state is that God has

---

12. 1 Peter 2:22 "Who did no sin, neither was guile found in his mouth:"

created two independent and separate jurisdictions, both of which are directly responsible to God. Today in America, we define separation of church and state as separation of God from the state. However, in scripture, civil magistrates are specifically called ministers of God.[13] This commandment is clear that God has given the civil magistrate a responsibility to constrain the evil of breaking the Sabbath, because God commands the foreigner not to work, and the only ones who have jurisdiction over the foreigner are the civil magistrates.

This is a picture of how even those who are outside of the church are to be blessed by the church. In a sense, they are sanctified by the church, but not in a justification sense. Justification is done solely through the belief in the Son of God. But in a temporal sense, a nation that applies scriptural principles to its ruling will be a great blessing to its people, even those who reject God. They are to be forced to stop working. They are to be forced to acknowledge at least with their actions that it is God who provides. They are to see the testimony to God's mercy and how He provides for His people by them following it. This will result in the nation more frequently making the morally correct choice. Rarely in history has a majority of the population had a credible profession of Christianity, but many times a majority generally followed God's law outwardly because the Christians were acting effectively as salt and light in the world. The Sabbath is a sanctified day for a sanctified people. When we allow the professing Christians among us to desecrate the Sabbath, we are testifying that we are not a people who have been set

---

13. Romans 13:6 " For for this cause pay ye tribute also: for they are God's ministers, attending continually upon this very thing."

apart by the almighty God. We wonder why people say that the reason they do not attend church is because it is filled with hypocrites. When we fail to keep the Sabbath, do we realize that their testimony is accurate?

God Sanctified from the World

The Sabbath is also a testimony that God is sanctified from this world. Jesus said that if His kingdom was of this world, He would have fought.[14] But His kingdom is not of this world. One of the ways we are to win the lost is to rest one day in seven. That is contrary to all worldly wisdom. The world says you can increase productivity by one seventh simply by cutting out that rest. In the eyes of the world, how can the person that rests one in seven days possibly be as productive as one who works all seven? But by resting on the seventh day, we are testifying that God is not establishing His kingdom the way that the world does. We are testifying that it is not the world that controls God, but that God controls the world. We are testifying that while we are given work to do by God, it is not our work that provides the increase. It is the sovereign God who is actively determining when the seed is put into the ground whether it will bear fruit. The Sabbath is about testifying that the things that we do to provide for ourselves, to take dominion, to baptize the nations and to teach them God's commandments, are secondary causes and not the primary cause of the increase. When we think that the fruit of those things will be greater if we do not rest on the Sabbath, we are testifying that the increase

---

14. John 18:36 " Jesus answered, My kingdom is not of this world: if my kingdom were of this world, then would my servants fight, that I should not be delivered to the Jews: but now is my kingdom not from hence."

of those activities is because of the strength of our hands, rather than God choosing to bless them. We come before God in prayer and ask Him to work in these areas and that is a good and proper thing to do, but then when we ignore His Sabbath we are testifying that we do not believe in the efficacy of those prayers.

The Work of Worship

There is work that is to be done on the Sabbath that also testifies to the transcendent God. But the work done on the Sabbath is not work in this world's sense of work, but it is the work of worship. It is laboring in prayer. The focus of the Sabbath is not even on the improvement of man. Yes, the worship service does have a great benefit to the growth of the holiness in the church and the edification of the body, but that is not the primary purpose of the Sabbath day. The primary purpose of the Sabbath is to commune with the husband of the church, the God through whom all things were created. It is a testimony that the focus of our lives is not our earthly citizenship, but our heavenly citizenship. When we violate the Sabbath, we are testifying that we are not looking forward to a heavenly country as our father Abraham did, rather we are satisfied with this earth. May it never be! God has promised good things to us, and the Sabbath rest with the people of God is to be a foretaste of the good things that God has promised in heaven. By our behavior on Sunday, we are proclaiming the state of our affections; whether our affections are mired in the things of this world, or if our true love is beyond this world, in heavenly places.

Free from Slavery to Sin

The Sabbath was also created by God to testify that it is He who sanctifies us and not we ourselves. In Deuteronomy, the second giving of the law, there is a change in the wording of the commandment:

And remember that thou wast a servant in the land of Egypt, and that the LORD thy God brought thee out thence through a mighty hand and by a stretched out arm: therefore the LORD thy God commanded thee to keep the sabbath day.[15]

There was clearly another purpose that God gave Israel for observing the Sabbath day besides a day of rest, and that is to remember that they were slaves and now are free. They were not freed by their own strength, but because God applied His strength in a very visible and active way. That is why they were to keep the Sabbath day. Is that not as applicable to us as it was to them? By God's grace, He delivered us from our slavery to sin. Just like the Israelites, we did not want to leave our slavery to sin when God first called us. We put up with the slavery for what we saw as its good benefits, but God plagued us with the effects of our sin until we feared Him, and then He led us out of our slavery. We are to remember the Sabbath day, because of the freedom that God gave us. Too often we look at the Sabbath and say it is enslavement. People say, "We are free in Christ. We are free from the curse of the law. How can God now tell us to keep the Sabbath?" Instead, we should understand that the reason we are to keep it is precisely because we have been freed from the slavery

---

15 Deuteronomy 5:15.

of sin and are now free to do God's will, instead of being enslaved to the powers of this world and the slavery of our flesh.

We are to keep the Sabbath day to remember that we
have been set free, but it is also a sign of that freedom:

> *Wherefore I caused them to go forth out of the land*
> *of Egypt, and brought them into the wilderness. And*
> *I gave them my statutes, and shewed them my judg-*
> *ments, which if a man do, he shall even live in them.*
> *Moreover also I gave them my sabbaths, to be a sign*
> *between me and them, that they might know that I am*
> *the LORD that sanctify them.* [16]

The Sabbath is intended to be a sign that God has taken us
out of Egypt. Scripturally, Egypt is a type of being dead in
our sins and trespasses.[17] Just as the Israelites in Egypt had a
cruel taskmaster that continually added to their burden, sin
is a cruel task master who is never satisfied, but is always in-
creasing his demands. But when God by His sovereign hand
reaches down and delivers us from our sin and brings us to
spiritual life, He then declares what we are to do and how we
are to live. If we continue to live in the same patterns as we
did before we were saved, we are testifying that we are still
enslaved by our sin. If we never have rest, we are testifying
that our master is not God who is a kind and gracious master. But we have been made free, and the Sabbath was given

---

16. Ezekiel 20:10-12.
17. 1 Corinthians 10:1-4 "Moreover, brethren, I would not that ye should be ignorant, how that all our fathers were under the cloud, and all passed through the
sea; And were all baptized unto Moses in the cloud and in the sea; And did all
eat the same spiritual meat; And did all drink the same spiritual drink: for they
drank of that spiritual Rock that followed them: and that Rock was Christ."

to us as a sign that we did not deliver ourselves from our sin, rather God delivered us.

Doctrines of Grace

When the doctrines of grace are ignored by the church, the violation of the Sabbath coincides. If we say that man chooses God without God initiating that choice, then why should we maintain a sign that God is the one who chose to set us aside? But if we believe that God personally chose before the foundation of the world that He would show mercy on the elect, even though we deserve eternal damnation, that He gave us life not because of any merit that He saw in us, then the Sabbath is a sign of the nature of our relationship with God. When we think that faith is not a gift of God, that we were wise enough to choose of ourselves, then it makes sense for us to ignore the Sabbath. As the American church has moved from the biblical doctrine which is frequently called Calvinism, we have also abandoned the Sabbath. We need to return to the understanding that we have no place to brag because it was God who saved us. A purpose of the Sabbath is a testimony that we understand that.

Continued Sanctification

It is also a sign not just that God justified us, but that He continues to sanctify us. On the Sabbath day, since it is a day to focus on the worship of God, we testify that we are sanctified through those practices that God has declared He will use to sanctify us.[18] If, for twenty-four hours every week, our focus is on worshiping the true God, that will

---

18. Ephesians 5:26 "That he might sanctify and cleanse it with the washing of water by the word,"

purify His people. The more that we are confronted by who God is and who we are, the more we understand the purity of God. When we recognize the purity of God, it highlights our impurity, and we repent and change our ways. When we recognize His mercy, we see how we have been merciless and we become merciful. When we see the love He had for us while we were His enemies, we start show love to our enemies. When we see how He loves His children, we do better at loving our brothers and sisters in the church. Our sanctification is a byproduct of our worship of God. God is kind and sanctifies us through understanding His true character and majesty. When we spend a day focused on the worship of God every week, by his grace we are changed in his presence.

A Witness to the World

That change is not just a sign to us, but it is a sign to the world around us. Since God declares that all who believe in Him are His ambassadors, the keeping of the Sabbath is a declaration that we recognize we are not made holy by our efforts, but we are made holy by the God who promises that He will complete the good work which He started in us.[19] When the people of the church are not keeping the Sabbath, instead of being a sign of hope to the world, they become a sign of hopelessness.

Everyone understands that their sin separates them from the God to whom every aspect of the world around them points, whether they will admit it or not.[20] When we tell them they must repent of their sin and turn to God, they

---

19. Philippians 1:6 "Being confident of this very thing, that he which hath begun a good work in you will perform it until the day of Jesus Christ:"
20. Romans 1

look at it as a hopeless task and they are right unless they understand that it is God who sanctifies them. They are only saved if God comes to them. God has a plan for how they will know that. God has given the Sabbath as a sign to His people so those around them can have hope that the God who sanctified the Christian can also sanctify them. When we violate the Sabbath and they see us turning from other areas of sin, instead of pointing them to the God who can save them, we are by our actions pointing them to their own strength. They already know that strength cannot deliver them. With our words, we can point them to the God who can save, but should our actions lead them to hopelessness?

When we testify that we have no need to keep the Sabbath, then our testimony is even more blunt and hopeless. What God has created to be a mercy to those around us, we have turned into a curse. Where God has designed into the pattern of a Christian's life a testimony to the God who cleanses from sin, we replace it with a claim of freedom from God's ways. While we say with our lips that God's ways are pleasant ways and all his paths are peace, we testify with our lives that they are really chains of iron that we need to break. The church of God needs to return to a testimony of the goodness of God and that it is His strength that saves us.

"Remember the Sabbath day to keep it holy"[21] needs to be our practice, and if we are to be a holy people serving a holy God, we must demonstrate it to the people around us.

---

21. Exodus 20:8

CHAPTER 4

The Defense

Whenever the Sabbath is discussed, there are always many arguments why we are no longer obligated to keep it. Some would argue that the Sabbath is gone because that was in the Old Testament era and we are now in the New Testament era. Some would argue that it was ceremonial law since it was pointing toward Christ and now has been fulfilled in Christ. And some would argue that Paul or Christ has explicitly eliminated the Sabbath, so it no longer applies.

Old Testament Law Specific to Israel

In looking at the scriptural commandment for justifying that the Sabbath has passed away, many look toward Deuteronomy 5:15:

And remember that thou wast a servant in the land of Egypt, and that the LORD thy God brought thee out thence through a mighty hand and by a stretched out arm: therefore the LORD thy God commanded thee to keep the sabbath day.

They say that since the Sabbath was to remember that you were a slave in Egypt, it must have applied to Israel alone. Of course, that is to ignore what Egypt represents throughout the Old Testament. The land of Egypt is a type of being enslaved by sin, being trapped in your inability to walk in righteousness and the need for God to deliver you. That is one of the things that the Sabbath is pointing to, that the mighty hand of God has taken us from slavery to freedom. To say that we should not keep the Sabbath is to say that we are not to remember that it was God who saved us. Remembering God's work is the center of worship. It is through remembering the work of God in our hearts that we come together to praise God, to desire to learn His ways, and to exhort each other to walk in them.

If the argument that Egypt was a type is not strong enough, the other giving of the Fourth Commandment in Exodus gives a different reason:

> *For in six days the LORD made heaven and earth, the sea, and all that in them is, and rested the seventh day: wherefore the LORD blessed the sabbath day, and hallowed it.*[1]

The Sabbath commandment cannot be specific to Israel because it is based upon something else. It is based upon the creation order, and therefore, everything has a duty to acknowledge that God is the Creator. Israel also knew its duty before the law was given. God commanded that they were to gather twice as much manna on the sixth day, so that they would not have to gather on the seventh. This happened before they reached Mount Sinai and were given the law.[2] One

---

1. Exodus 20:11.
2. Exodus 16:4-6 "Then said the LORD unto Moses, Behold, I will rain bread from heaven for you; and the people shall go out and gather a certain rate every

of the things that unbelievers will be judged for on the last day is their rejection of the Sabbath. They have not acknowledged their Creator, they have not done their reasonable service that is required by the truth. Instead, they have served the god of this world. The view that we are no longer bound by the slavery of the Law and we can work on the Sabbath is actually a testimony that we are still serving the god of this world. The god of this world says that the only way you will have those things that you need is to provide them by the strength of your own hand. The true God says that all things proceed from His hand, so we are to seek first the kingdom of God and His righteousness, and all these things shall be added to us.[3] By observing a day of rest, we are testifying that it is God who provides for us. Even when a seed is planted in the ground, it only comes up as a plant by the will of God. The rain falls from the sky only by the will of God. We cannot provide anything for ourselves. The day of rest is to testify that it is God who has been upholding the world until now and it is our responsibility to walk righteously before Him.

But God Himself is clear that it is not just Israel that is to keep His Sabbath:

> *Blessed is the man that doeth this, and the son of man that layeth hold on it; that keepeth the sabbath from polluting it, and keepeth his hand from doing any evil. Neither let the son of the stranger, that hath joined*

---

day, that I may prove them, whether they will walk in my law, or no. And it shall come to pass, that on the sixth day they shall prepare that which they bring in; and it shall be twice as much as they gather daily. And Moses and Aaron said unto all the children of Israel, At even, then ye shall know that the LORD hath brought you out from the land of Egypt:"

3. Matthew 6:33.

*himself to the LORD, speak, saying, The LORD hath
utterly separated me from his people: neither let the
eunuch say, Behold, I am a dry tree. For thus saith the
LORD unto the eunuchs that keep my sabbaths, and
choose the things that please me, and take hold of my
covenant; Even unto them will I give in mine house
and within my walls a place and a name better than
of sons and of daughters: I will give them an everlasting name, that shall not be cut off. Also the sons of the
stranger, that join themselves to the LORD, to serve
him, and to love the name of the LORD, to be his servants, every one that keepeth the sabbath from polluting it, and taketh hold of my covenant; Even them will
I bring to my holy mountain, and make them joyful
in my house of prayer: their burnt offerings and their
sacrifices shall be accepted upon mine altar; for mine
house shall be called an house of prayer for all people.*[4]

God specifically says that the son of man that lays hold on
God's salvation keeps from polluting the Sabbath and keeps
his hand from evil. No Christian would argue that being a
friend of Christ is not about obeying His commandments,
because Christ explicitly said so.[5] When we are saved, we
repent and turn from our sin. In other words, we keep our
hand from evil. Why then do we reject the first qualification
of those sons of men who have received salvation? Saved
people are deliberate in choosing to not pollute the Sabbath.
As with all of the commands of God, we always fall short, but

---

4.   Isaiah 56:2-7.
5.   John 15:14 "Ye are my friends, if ye do whatsoever I command you."

that is far different from intentionally ignoring the Sabbath laws that God has commanded us to obey.

Continuing in the Isaiah passage, God talks about the stranger and eunuch that join themselves to the Lord. If they do those things that He has commanded, specifically not polluting the Sabbath day and keeping our hand from doing evil, then He will give them a name better than of sons and daughters. He will give them an eternal name which will not be cut off. Loving the name of God manifests itself through serving God and keeping His Sabbaths. That is how the people that are not cut off from the eternal house of God behave. They come with joy. Even the eunuch who was not allowed in the earthly temple because of his blemish is acceptable to God in His true house.[6] This cannot be referring to the earthly temple, because of the statement that eunuchs will be allowed into the temple. God does not contradict Himself, but the physical metaphor of the temple is to teach us to be a perfect representative of the eternal temple where God dwells. It is clear that it could not be referring to laws that are specific to Israel.

Ceremonial Law

All of the ceremonial laws which were given to Israel were fulfilled in Christ. We are no longer to kill a Passover sacrifice. Even the Jews recognize that it is not possible to do so since the destruction of the temple. We are allowed to eat

---

6. Leviticus 21:18-20 "For whatsoever man he be that hath a blemish, he shall not approach: a blind man, or a lame, or he that hath a flat nose, or any thing superfluous, Or a man that is brokenfooted, or brokenhanded, Or crookbackt, or a dwarf, or that hath a blemish in his eye, or be scurvy, or scabbed, or hath his stones broken;" Deuteronomy 23:1 "He that is wounded in the stones, or hath his privy member cut off, shall not enter into the congregation of the LORD."

the food of a gentile as God revealed to Peter before he went to the centurion's house, because those things were types of things that have now been fulfilled. But the Sabbath has not been abrogated, because the earthly rest that God has given us is still a moral good. We do have a different kind of rest because we can rest in Christ, but we do not have the full rest that comes in eternity with God. In heaven we will not have to work against our flesh, we will not have to fight enemies of the cross of Jesus Christ, we will not have to teach each other the things of God because we will know in full. The work that we have been given to do in the Great Commission will be finished and the church will be at its fulfilled rest. If we think that rest is fulfilled now, we have forgotten the promise that we will be raised incorruptible and enter into the eternal rest of heaven.

> *And I heard a voice from heaven saying unto me, Write, Blessed are the dead which die in the Lord from henceforth: Yea, saith the Spirit, that they may rest from their labours; and their works do follow them.* [7]

We have lost the hope of a better world if we think that Christ has already fulfilled the final rest. Through His death, burial and resurrection, Christ has guaranteed to give us that final rest, but it has not been fulfilled yet. He has sealed us for that rest through the Holy Spirit, but it is still a promise to the people of God.

Christ Abrogated the Sabbath

Another way that people attempt to refute the Sabbath is by claiming that Christ rebuked the Pharisees because they

---

7. Revelation 14:13.

kept the Sabbath. What they do not understand is that Jesus was clarifying the ways that the Pharisees had twisted the Sabbath and invented new laws. Jesus was not abrogating the Sabbath. He was just removing the corrupt trappings that the Jews and Pharisees had covered it with.

Consider Matthew 12:1-8:

> *At that time Jesus went on the sabbath day through the corn; and his disciples were an hungred, and began to pluck the ears of corn, and to eat. But when the Pharisees saw it, they said unto him, Behold, thy disciples do that which is not lawful to do upon the sabbath day. But he said unto them, Have ye not read what David did, when he was an hungred, and they that were with him; How he entered into the house of God, and did eat the shewbread, which was not lawful for him to eat, neither for them which were with him, but only for the priests? Or have ye not read in the law, how that on the sabbath days the priests in the temple profane the sabbath, and are blameless? But I say unto you, That in this place is one greater than the temple. But if ye had known what this meaneth, I will have mercy, and not sacrifice, ye would not have condemned the guiltless. For the Son of man is Lord even of the sabbath day.*

In this passage, the Pharisees accuse Jesus' disciples of breaking the Sabbath by eating corn, or grain as other translations render it. The disciples were picking grain, rubbing the chaff off of it in their hands, and eating it on the Sabbath. The Pharisees said that they were breaking the Sabbath by working. The Rabbis had decided from study of the scriptures that there were thirty-nine different actions which were considered working.[8] Since the disciples were picking grain, the Pharisees said that they were reaping, threshing, winnowing, etc. as they ate the grain. Jesus used the example of David when he ate the showbread that was reserved for the Levites alone, which showed that if righteousness came by the way which the Pharisees believed, through good works, even David was unacceptable in the sight of God. Jesus also pointed out that the Levites were specifically commanded to do work on the Sabbath based upon the Pharisees' understanding of work. How then could the Levites not be breaking the law?

The Pharisees thought they could perfectly understand and dictate what should be done on the Sabbath. Jesus declared that is not the case, rather that they were hypocrites.

Jesus then declared the truth, that He is the Lord of the Sabbath. He does not say that He is the Lord of something that is shortly going to pass away, rather He says that as the Lord of the Sabbath, He has perfect understanding of what should and should not be done on the Sabbath. He specifically rebuked them by saying that if they knew Him, they would not have condemned the guiltless, His disciples. This is not a passage about the elimination of the Sabbath, but about properly understanding that the Sabbath is not about working versus rest, rather it is about sanctification of our work and rest.

Another passage that is used to support the claim that Jesus has abolished the Sabbath is Luke 13:14-15:

---

8. John Barclay *The Talmud* (London: John Murray, Albemarle Street, 1878) Retrieved from *Google Books*. Web. November 4th, 2009 p. 92.

And the ruler of the synagogue answered with indignation, because that Jesus had healed on the sabbath day, and said unto the people, There are six days in which men ought to work: in them therefore come and be healed, and not on the sabbath day. The Lord then answered him, and said, Thou hypocrite, doth not each one of you on the sabbath loose his ox or his ass from the stall, and lead him away to watering?

Again, when Christ healed he was not breaking the Sabbath. It could not be, otherwise He was not sinless and was not the sinless lamb who is able to cover our sins. They made a false accusation against Him, which their own behavior testified they could not follow. When the claim is made that Jesus eliminated the Sabbath because He broke it by healing, that argument is agreeing with the Pharisees who misunderstood the law. Nowhere in the law are acts of healing or mercy forbidden. Jesus honored the Sabbath day by showing God's mercy on that day through the healing.

Paul Abrogated the Sabbath

The last argument about the termination of the Sabbath is that Paul explicitly eliminated the Sabbath in Colossians:

Blotting out the handwriting of ordinances that was against us, which was contrary to us, and took it out of the way, nailing it to his cross; And having spoiled principalities and powers, he made a shew of them openly, triumphing over them in it. Let no man therefore judge you in meat, or in drink, or in respect of an holyday, or of the new moon, or of the sabbath days:

Which are a shadow of things to come; but the body is of Christ. [9]

This is important to consider carefully, because at first look the interpretation seems clear. The Sabbaths are just like meat and drink. As those laws had their purpose for a time to point to something greater, so the Sabbath day is gone because it pointed to Christ.

The first thing to consider is the use of the language. The word "days" was added by the translators. The word in Greek is literally "Sabbaths." In the Mosaic law, there are three Sabbaths: the weekly Sabbath, the seventh year Sabbath and the Jubilee year Sabbath which is the seventh Sabbath year.

The seventh year and the Jubilee Sabbaths were fulfilled in Christ because they were always about pointing to freedom. Debts were required to be forgiven, slaves were to be set free, the land was not planted so that the poor and the beasts of the fields could come and eat,[10] and liberty was to be proclaimed by returning the land to whom God had given it.[11] Through Christ, we are free from our debt to the law.[12] We are also set free from our enslavement to sin.[13] Christ came for the poor and lowly in spirit, and even the dogs of

---

9. Colossians 2:14-17.

10. Exodus 23:11"But the seventh year thou shalt let it rest and lie still; that the poor of thy people may eat: and what they leave the beasts of the field shall eat. In like manner thou shalt deal with thy vineyard, and with thy oliveyard."

11. Leviticus 25:10 "And ye shall hallow the fiftieth year, and proclaim liberty throughout all the land unto all the inhabitants thereof: it shall be a jubile unto you; and ye shall return every man unto his possession, and ye shall return every man unto his family."

12. Galatians 5:3 " For I testify again to every man that is circumcised, that he is a debtor to do the whole law."

13. Romans 6:6 "Knowing this, that our old man is crucified with him, that the body of sin might be destroyed, that henceforth we should not serve sin."

the Gentiles.[14] All the things that those Sabbaths have pointed to were fulfilled in Christ.

But the Christian weekly Sabbath, which is called the Lord's Day, the call to remember our Creator and our Redeemer, is now more of a significant call than ever for the Christian, because we have a greater understanding of the gospel. The other Sabbath that passed away was the Jewish weekly Sabbath, the Sabbath that was set every year by the fifteenth day of the first month has also been fulfilled by Jesus Christ on the cross. That weekly Sabbath was to remember being freed from Egypt. We no longer have a requirement to remember that event, because we do not have just the shadows like the Jews. We keep the Lord's Day to remember Christ's death on the cross. To have a weekly celebration of the Jewish Sabbath is as meaningless to us as celebrating the Feast of Weeks rather than the accomplished fact that the Holy Spirit actually has circumcised our hearts.

When Paul commands them not to judge one another based on these clearly ceremonial laws, he is also not saying that it is wrong for some to practice them. Paul was writing during a time of transition from the Old Covenant and temple worship to the new practices that come from deeper understanding of how things were fulfilled through Christ. Paul is admonishing them not to sit in judgment related to the things that were ceremonial. Taking a Nazarite vow was also passing away, but in the New Testament we see Paul himself practicing that ceremony.[15] After the destruction of

---

14. Matthew 15:27 "And she said, Truth, Lord: yet the dogs eat of the crumbs which fall from their masters' table."

15. Acts 18:18 "And Paul after this tarried there yet a good while, and then took his leave of the brethren, and sailed thence into Syria, and with him Priscilla and

the temple, that practice could no longer be continued. It was not appropriate to judge based on following those commandments, because God had commanded them to the Jews, so the laws were righteous. But at the same time, because their ceremonial aspect had been fulfilled, they were passing away. So some of them may have been practicing the Jewish Sabbath along with the Lord's Day, because they saw the commandments in scripture still applying to them. But that is no reason for us to think that the Lord's Day is passed away as well when Paul refers to celebrating the first day of the week multiple times elsewhere.

Another scripture that is used to refute the continuation of the Sabbath is Romans 14:5-6:

One person esteems one day above another; another esteems every day alike. Let each be fully convinced in his own mind. He who observes the day, observes it to the Lord; and he who does not observe the day, to the Lord he does not observe it. He who eats, eats to the Lord, for he gives God thanks; and he who does not eat, to the Lord he does not eat, and gives God thanks.

Clearly this passage of scripture is speaking of days for observation, because it is in the context of what you eat and drink. All of the set Jewish feasts were centered around food.

I will also cause all her mirth to cease, her feast days, her new moons, and her sabbaths, and all her solemn feasts. [16]

So again the Romans passage is probably best understood

Aquila; having shorn his head in Cenchrea: for he had a vow."
16. Hosea 2:11.

as a transitional passage between the Old Testament system of worship and the New Testament system. We know that Paul still desired to celebrate the Feast of Pentecost from Acts 20:16. Earlier in that chapter, we are told that Paul, even though he was in a hurry to get to Jerusalem, stayed in Troas until the first day of the week so he could celebrate the Lord's Day with the disciples in that city, which testifies that He saw the Lord's Day as a specific day of the week on which to worship God. This interpretation of the Romans 14 passage is consistent with Paul's recorded actions. We see Paul continuing other aspects of the ceremonial law such as taking a Nazarite vow. One thing that this text does not lend itself to is to make this an absolute repudiation of the Sabbath, since the term for Sabbath is not even specifically referenced. To use it to eliminate one of the ten commandments is to use an unclear passage to abrogate many more specific passages. An important hermeneutical principle is that all scriptural texts can be harmonized. So when they appear to conflict, the clear passages must be used to determine a proper interpretation of the unclear. Since this passage does not refer to the Sabbath, the other clear texts of scripture are authoritative in our understanding of this verse.

In defending from scripture the continuance of the Sabbath, one question we should ask ourselves is why we would want this blessed day to go away. God has called us to come and rejoice with Him on this day. To set aside the cares of this world and seek the blessings of being part of the kingdom of God should be something that every Christian desires. We should not be looking at reasons to free ourselves from the bonds of the Sabbath because they are bonds of love. They are the bonds which are intended to bind Christ with His bride.

CHAPTER 5

The Judgment

Before we consider the kindness and mercy of God in giving us the Sabbath, we should start first with understanding how God judges those who do not keep the Sabbath. In looking at God's judgment, we need to start by understanding that:

> *The fear of the LORD is the beginning of wisdom: and the knowledge of the holy is understanding.*[1]

The United States is currently a nation that is under judgment. Not just the nation, but the church as well for judgment begins in the house of God.[2] By most cultural measures, those who call themselves Christians have lives that are little different than the world around them. When we look at the curses that are in Deuteronomy 28, where God tells what will come upon the people if they do not keep His commands, we need to recognize how many of the curses our nation is experiencing. Certainly not all of them, but a considerable

---

1. Proverbs 9:10.
2. 1 Peter 4:17 "For the time is come that judgment must begin at the house of God: and if it first begin at us, what shall the end be of them that obey not the gospel of God?"

number. "Cursed shall be the fruit of thy body"[3] - we see that somewhere between eighty and ninety percent of the children growing up in the church are lost.[4] The church is losing ground in virtually every cultural fight it engages in, whether it is sodomite marriage or abortion. "The Lord shall cause thee to be smitten before thine enemies:"[5] - We have become a people who, when we rise up against our enemies, instead of believing that we will be victorious, are hopeful that we may be able to delay our defeat. We are far from having received the fullness of God's cursing and the people outside of the church have been cursed in far more serious ways, but we should consider seriously what God has done to His people in the past when He has cursed them and why He said that He cursed them.

The History of Judah

When we think about the commandment to keep the Sabbath holy as a sign that we are a holy people that God has set apart for sanctification, we need to recognize that God does chasten His people when they disobey His commandments, both individually and corporately. To understand how fully He will discipline His people, we need to examine the history of Judah and how it ties to breaking the Sabbath.

Captivity

While Solomon was king, he reigned over all of the

---

3. Deuteronomy 28:18.
4. "According to researchers, between 70 and 88 percent of Christian teens are leaving church by their second year of college." Baucham, Voddie T. Jr. *Family Driven Faith* (Weaton, Illoinois: Crossway Books, 2007) p. 80.
5. Deuteronomy 28:25.

land that had been originally promised to Abraham.[6] After he died, God used the cruelty of his son to split off the ten northern tribes of Israel into the nation of Israel. Only the tribes of Judah and Benjamin continued in the kingdom of Judah. Israel immediately became apostate through the work of Jeroboam when he put two golden calves at opposite ends of Israel to try to convince them not to go up to the house of God to worship.[7] God then sent the Assyrians and other nations to destroy them. However, most of Judah continued to worship at the temple, sometimes more faithfully and sometimes less faithfully. Finally, God sent the Babylonians to take Israel captive, which happened first in 606 BC,[8] and Daniel was part of this group of captives taken to Babylon. The next invasion was led by Nebuchadnezzar in 597 BC[9] when he removed the king who had rebelled and installed his brother as king and renamed him Zedekiah, which means "The justice of the Lord." Zedekiah continued to pursue evil.

For through the anger of the LORD it came to pass in Jerusalem and Judah, until he had cast them out from

---

6. 1 Kings 4:21" And Solomon reigned over all kingdoms from the river unto the land of the Philistines, and unto the border of Egypt: they brought presents, and served Solomon all the days of his life."

7. 1 Kings 12:27-29 "If this people go up to do sacrifice in the house of the LORD at Jerusalem, then shall the heart of this people turn again unto their lord, even unto Rehoboam king of Judah, and they shall kill me, and go again to Rehoboam king of Judah. Whereupon the king took counsel, and made two calves of gold, and said unto them, It is too much for you to go up to Jerusalem: behold thy gods, O Israel, which brought thee up out of the land of Egypt. And he set the one in Bethel, and the other put he in Dan."

8. Floyd Nolen Jones *The Chronology of the Old Testament* (Green Forest, AR: Master Books, 2005) p. 280.

9. *Ibid.*

his presence, that Zedekiah rebelled against the king of Babylon. [10]

To fulfill God's justice, Zedekiah rebelled against the king of Babylon and for the third time, Nebuchadnezzar came in 586 BC[11] and destroyed the temple along with the gates of Jerusalem. For the third time, a group of people were taken captive back to Babylon, but this time, the only people that were left fled to Egypt and the land was completely desolate. So why did all this happen?

> *And they burnt the house of God, and brake down the wall of Jerusalem, and burnt all the palaces thereof with fire, and destroyed all the goodly vessels thereof. And them that had escaped from the sword carried he away to Babylon; where they were servants to him and his sons until the reign of the kingdom of Persia: To fulfil the word of the LORD by the mouth of Jeremiah, until the land had enjoyed her sabbaths: for as long as she lay desolate she kept sabbath, to fulfil threescore and ten years.* [12]

The word of the Lord was fulfilled and Judah was destroyed for not keeping the Sabbath. The Sabbath that this passage refers to are the Sabbath years which God set aside so that the land could rest, which the Israelites had never obeyed. In other passages, God does list other reasons why they were destroyed, but this was the one God used to determine the length of the punishment. God destroyed them as a na-

---

10. 2 Kings 24:20.
11. *The Chronology of the Old Testament*, p. 280.
12 2 Chronicles 36:19-21.

tion, killing many of them by the sword, famine and disease, because they had violated the Sabbath year.

The Oath

Just as the captivity happened in three phases, so did the restoration starting in 536 BC[13] led by Zerubbabel,[14] followed by Ezra and the last group by Nehemiah around 520 BC.[15] After the third group was led back, Ezra opened the book of the law and the people repented and covenanted together to obey God's law to avoid God's wrath falling on them again.

> *And the rest of the people, the priests, the Levites, the porters, the singers, the Nethinims, and all they that had separated themselves from the people of the lands unto the law of God, their wives, their sons, and their daughters, every one having knowledge, and having understanding; They clave to their brethren, their nobles, and entered into a curse, and into an oath, to walk in God's law, which was given by Moses the servant of God, and to observe and do all the commandments of the LORD our Lord, and his judgments and his statutes; And that we would not give our daughters unto the people of the land, nor take their daughters for our sons: And if the people of the land bring ware or any victuals on the sabbath day to sell, that we would not buy it of them on the sabbath, or on the holy day: and that we would leave the seventh year, and the exaction of every debt.* [16]

---

13. *The Chronology of the Old Testament*, p. 280.
14. Ezra 2:2 "Which came with Zerubbabel ..."
15. *The Chronology of the Old Testament*, p. 280.
16. Nehemiah 10:28-31.

Notice how they swore to walk in God's law, but then they specified only three laws on which they put emphasis: not taking foreign wives, not buying and selling on the Sabbath and letting the land rest the Sabbath year. They understood that special emphasis needed to be put on keeping the Sabbath day because it was one of the reasons that God had destroyed them seventy years before.

Nehemiah's Reform

Of course, it did not take them long before they violated their oath. Nehemiah went back to Artaxerxes, the king of Babylon, because he was his cup bearer for about twelve years. When he returned, all of the people had gone back to the same practices that they had sworn an oath that they would abandon. They had married foreign wives, and had moved Tobiah, one of the leaders that had attempted to prevent the rebuilding of the wall, into the temple itself. In addition, when Nehemiah looked on the Sabbath, he saw the people of Judah violating every aspect of the Sabbath in their practices. Buying and selling, working servants and forcing their animals to work, he saw it all.[17] His response is not that it is a shame that they are doing so, his response is, as the civil magistrate, to constrain their evil. Undoubtedly, he recognized that God had judged and had promised to judge people for violating the Sabbath day. Specifically, in Jeremiah, God

---

17. Nehemiah 13:15-16 "In those days saw I in Judah some treading wine presses on the sabbath, and bringing in sheaves, and lading asses; as also wine, grapes, and figs, and all manner of burdens, which they brought into Jerusalem on the sabbath day: and I testified against them in the day wherein they sold victuals. There dwelt men of Tyre also therein, which brought fish, and all manner of ware, and sold on the sabbath unto the children of Judah, and in Jerusalem. "

promised that He would destroy them again, if they once again resorted to the same evil practices.

Thus saith the LORD; Take heed to yourselves, and bear no burden on the sabbath day, nor bring it in by the gates of Jerusalem; Neither carry forth a burden out of your houses on the sabbath day, neither do ye any work, but hallow ye the sabbath day, as I commanded your fathers. But they obeyed not, neither inclined their ear, but made their neck stiff, that they might not hear, nor receive instruction. And it shall come to pass, if ye diligently hearken unto me, saith the LORD, to bring in no burden through the gates of this city on the sabbath day, but hallow the sabbath day, to do no work therein; Then shall there enter into the gates of this city kings and princes sitting upon the throne of David, riding in chariots and on horses, they, and their princes, the men of Judah, and the inhabitants of Jerusalem: and this city shall remain for ever. And they shall come from the cities of Judah, and from the places about Jerusalem, and from the land of Benjamin, and from the plain, and from the mountains, and from the south, bringing burnt offerings, and sacrifices, and meat offerings, and incense, and bringing sacrifices of praise, unto the house of the LORD. But if ye will not hearken unto me to hallow the sabbath day, and not to bear a burden, even entering in at the gates of Jerusalem on the sabbath day; then will I kindle a fire in the gates thereof, and it shall devour the palaces of Jerusalem, and it shall not be quenched. [18]

As the civil magistrate, Nehemiah recognized his responsibility to act, recognizing that it is God who defends the city, and he stopped the evil practices.

The Magistrate's Responsibility

To our modern ears, it is odd to think that the civil magistrate should be acting in what is clearly a religious matter. But even a few years ago this was not the case. It was considered right and normal. The purpose of the civil magistrate is to constrain evil and God clearly says that breaking the Sabbath is evil. The purpose of the civil magistrate is to defend the city. They were given the sword. God says that He will exhibit His wrath for things that defile the land like breaking the Sabbath, taking His name in vain, worshiping idols, spilling innocent blood and many other things that He promises He will avenge on the people. A civil magistrate as a minister of God[19] has as much responsibility to turn the people away from those practices that are an affront to God as to constrain those practices which directly affect other men. We tend to think that doing something against man is evil and should be constrained, but to violate a commandment that does not affect other men, but is just between a man and God, should be left to the freedom of conscience. However, that is not the scriptural position. Scripture has

---

18. Jeremiah 17:21-27.
19. Romans 13:4 "For he is the minister of God to thee for good. But if thou do that which is evil, be afraid; for he beareth not the sword in vain: for he is the minister of God, a revenger to execute wrath upon him that doeth evil."

defined these things as evil and God has given the sword to the state for the constraining of evil.

Death Penalty

God even commanded what the punishment should be for the violation of the Sabbath:

> And while the children of Israel were in the wilderness, they found a man that gathered sticks upon the sabbath day. And they that found him gathering sticks brought him unto Moses and Aaron, and unto all the congregation. And they put him in ward, because it was not declared what should be done to him. And the LORD said unto Moses, The man shall be surely put to death: all the congregation shall stone him with stones without the camp. And all the congregation brought him without the camp, and stoned him with stones, and he died; as the LORD commanded Moses.[20]

Putting aside the argument whether the punishment should still be death for violating the Sabbath, God is clearly saying in this passage that the crime is that serious. In our society today virtually everyone considers that murder is a horrible crime that people should be punished for, but murder is only wrong because God commands men not to murder. We should consider that God puts the Sabbath on the same level as murder. Nehemiah did not put all of the people to death probably because he would not have been able to convince the people to stone the offenders as they were all doing the same thing. But still, Nehemiah did see it as his responsibility to enforce the law of God.

---

20. Numbers 15:32-36.

When we consider that, in our culture, the civil magistrate typically does not act in this area, we should recognize that the civil government walks in the light given to it by the church. The way to fix the problem is not to elect officials at the highest level, who will enforce this position when they get into office without expressing that opinion. Most governments that God appoints are similar to the people they are constraining. Just as Nehemiah could not impose the death penalty on all of the people violating the Sabbath, because the people would not concur, we should not think that if the people do not understand the need, the government should impose it by fiat. Instead, the church has the obligation to show forth the light of the gospel, including that God grants to all people a day of rest, even those in rebellion to Him. The church should be expressing the truth and goodness of what God has given to us. If we start to walk in that light, the darkness will flee from that light. If we are faithful to uphold the Sabbath, the civil magistrate will start enforcing it. Judgment begins in the house of God.[21]

Our Punishment

When we consider the punishment that God has afflicted upon His people for breaking the Sabbath, we should consider what He might choose to do to the church today, when we so blatantly disregard it. God punished Israel for their violation, both because it was against His law, and because it was a sign of general lawlessness among those people who were called by His name. Today, we are in that same

---

21. 1 Peter 4:17 "For the time is come that judgment must begin at the house of God: and if it first begin at us, what shall the end be of them that obey not the gospel of God?"

circumstance. We cry that we are free in Christ and we have been freed from the yoke of bondage, without considering at the same time, that we have been given the perfect law of liberty. God's people obey His commandments. This is a sign that they are his sons. If your son is constantly rebelling against everything that you tell him, he does not stop being your son. However, a righteous parent will not spare the rod in that circumstance. Similarly, our perfect Father in heaven will not fail to chasten us if we despise His ways instead of delighting in them. With Judah, He chastened them to the point that only a small remnant remained. May we repent, before the immutable and unchangeable God does the same to us.

CHAPTER 6

The History

For us to understand how out of step we are with the historical church, we need to consider and understand how the Sabbath has been viewed by the church, especially since the Reformation. With the Reformation came a renewal of the belief in the Sufficiency of Scripture: that scripture is the infallible guide for every good work. How we spend one seventh of our time is certainly a significant good work because we are God's servants, and all our time is His. If we misuse that time, we should expect to be disciplined by God because we are commanded to redeem the time for the days are full of evil.[1] God has told us how our weeks are to be guided.

Those Who have Gone Before

When we consider previous generations of the church and their views, we need to consider them in the correct light. Just because the church traditionally has held a different view, does not give that view authority. Jesus warned us about adopting vain traditions of men and how those traditions can be a snare to us.[2] But on the other hand, we should

---

1   Ephesians 5:16 "Redeeming the time, because the days are evil."

2.   Mark 7:6-8 "He answered and said unto them, Well hath Esaias prophesied of

be equally cautious about adopting a view just because it is new. The culture we have grown up in is based upon an evolutionary worldview, and we have been taught by that culture to believe that newer things are inherently better than older things.

Instead, we need to take the balanced approach of showing respect to the memories of those who have gone before us. The faith that we have had handed to us has been passed from generation to generation by these men. For us to disdain their work is to dishonor our fathers in the faith, but we must remember that they were just men. Many of them were more brilliant lights to the church than anyone present in this age. We must stand on the shoulders of those who have gone before us, and not ignore their wisdom to inflate our own pride. To listen to the godly men who have gone before us is to testify to the continuity of the church and the continuing efficacy of the Holy Spirit working in the church. We must understand that the Sabbath has always been a battleground in the church. Breaking the Sabbath was a continual problem in Israel and the desire to disobey continues to be widespread in the church. But when we look to the example of Godly men that have been a great blessing to the church, there is a large level of unanimity throughout church history.

Early Church
Most of the early church practiced the Christian

---

you hypocrites, as it is written, This people honoureth me with their lips, but their heart is far from me. Howbeit in vain do they worship me, teaching for doctrines the commandments of men. For laying aside the commandment of God, ye hold the tradition of men, as the washing of pots and cups: and many other such like things ye do."

Sabbath. Saint Chrysostom, who lived from AD 347 – 407, said:

> *"You ought not, when you have retired from the church assembly, to involve yourselves in engagements contrary to the exercise with which you have been occupied, but immediately on coming home read the Sacred Scriptures, and call together the family, wife and children, to confer about the things that have been spoken, and after they have been more deeply and thoroughly impressed upon the mind, then proceed to attend to such matters as are necessary for this life."* [3]

The Council of Laodicea, in AD 364, said, *"A Christian shall not stop work on the Sabbath, but on the Lord's Day."*[4] They were recognizing that Christians should cease from their work and rest in the Lord. They were especially saying that the Sabbath has switched from the seventh to the first day of the week.[5]

The Reformed Church

The position of the historic reformed church, both Credobaptist and Paedobaptist,[6] has been the continuation of the commandment for Christians to turn from their own pleasures and to do God's pleasure on the Sabbath - His

3. J. N. Andrews and L. R. Conradi *History of the Sabbath and First Day of the Week* (Washington D. C.: Review & Herald Publishing Association, 1912) Retrieved from Google Books. Web. November 6th, 2009 p. 428-429

4. Philip Schaff ed. *The Nicene and Post Nicene Fathers*, Series 2, Volume 14, Synod of Laodicea, Canon XXIX Web. http://www.ccel.org/ccel/schaff/npnf214.viii.vii.iii.xxxiv.html Retrieved November 6th, 2009.

5. For a discussion of why the day changed, see Chapter 6, *The Day*.

6. Credobaptists are those who hold the position that baptism should only be administered to those who have professed faith. Paedobaptists are those who hold the position that the children of believers should be baptized.

holy day. For instance, from the Second London Baptist Confession of Faith:

> *The sabbath is then kept holy unto the Lord, when men, after a due preparing of their hearts, and ordering their common affairs aforehand, do not only observe an holy rest all day, from their own works, words and thoughts, about their worldly employment and recreations, but are also taken up the whole time in the public and private exercises of his worship, and in the duties of necessity and mercy.*[7]

We need to understand that this is the historic position of the faithful church. They believed that the fourth commandment as given in Exodus 20 and Deuteronomy 5 has not passed away. Later in this book, we will discuss how the Sabbath has changed from pointing back to the exodus from Egypt to our exodus from slavery of sin into the freedom of Christ. The idea of one day being set apart in seven has been considered binding to all people at all times. It is the duty that we owe our Creator. To ignore it is to declare that God is a horrible taskmaster who will not give his servants a day of rest.

Calvin's Position on the Sabbath

Many people say that the Reformers rejected the Sabbath because of a story that has been in circulation for many years about the great reformer John Calvin. The story is usually told that when John Knox came to Geneva, the first thing that he did was look for Calvin. When Knox came to his house, he found him out in the back lawn bowling. He

---

7. *Second London Baptist Confession*, Chapter 22:8.

was very surprised because it was a Sabbath afternoon. The problem with this story is that there is no contemporaneous evidence that it is true. But even if it was, all it would show is that Calvin sinned according to his stated position. This story arose out of the desire for unrighteous mammon, so that the name of a great man of God who was a true blessing to the church has been defamed.

When the story is footnoted, it leads back to a book written by a man named Robert Cox in 1860. However, the book that he wrote called The *Whole Doctrine of Calvin about the Sabbath* does not actually contain the story that is attributed to it. The purpose of his books can be readily discerned from the title of the first chapter of another book he wrote: *A Plea for Sunday Trains on the Edinburgh and Glasgow Railway.*[8] The whole story is that Robert Cox was a shareholder in the Edinburgh and Glasgow Railway and was leading a drive to change the law about work on the Lord's Day so that the railway would make more money. He never referred to the bowling story in any of this writings, but people started to footnote the story back to his anti-Sabbath book. Because there is no record of the story until more than two hundred years after Calvin's death, a story is widely accepted as fact because of men's desire to deny their duty toward God to honor His Sabbath.[9]

John Calvin's position according to his own writings is very clear. Since he was not the civil magistrate, it is likely

---

8.   Richard Cox *Sabbath Laws and Sabbath Duties*, (Edinburgh: Maclachlan and Stewart, 1853) Retrieved from Google Books. Web. October 20th, 2009 p. 1

9.   Chris Coldwell *Calvin in the Hands of the Philistines: Or, Did Calvin Bowl on the Sabbath?* Web. http://www.fpcr.org/blue_banner_articles/calvin_bowls. htm Accessed October 19th, 2009.

that certain practices of which he would disapprove were taking place on the Lord's Day. Frequently, the civil magistrates would encourage participation in martial events on the Sabbath, since the Lord's Day was the only day that everyone was not at work. Because this was an era where every able-bodied man was considered part of the militia, the Lord's Day would be used as the day to train in the arts of war. But that was not John Calvin's position. Calvin specifically spoke against playing sports on the Sabbath. He said in his 34th sermon on Deuteronomy in 15:44:

> *If we spend the Lord's day in making good cheer, and in playing and gaming, is that a good honouring of God? Nay, is it not a mockery, yea and a very unhallowing of his name?*[10]

So if he did bowl on the Lord's Day, it was contrary to his stated position and we should assume that his congregation would have called him to repentance.

Samuel Rutherford

A century later the position of the church had not changed. There is a story that is much better documented about Samuel Rutherford, one of the greatest Scottish theologians. Early in his ministry, just after being appointed to preach at a small rural parish in 1627, he learned that many of his parishioners would play football on the Lord's Day after the morning worship services. When he found out where they went for their sport, he went there and called down

---

10. Primus "John H. Calvin and the Puritan Sabbath: A Comparative Study" in *Exploring The Heritage Of John Calvin: Essays In Honor Of John Bratt*, ed. David E. Holwerda (Grand Rapids: Baker, 1976). p. 68-69

curses from heaven upon them for dishonoring the Sabbath. He pointed to three massive stones that stood overlooking the field. He referred to Joshua[11] and said these stones stood as witnesses against them. The moment was so powerful that two hundred years later, those stones were still known as Rutherford's witnesses.[12] In the seventeenth century they understood that God will curse those who break His commandments regarding the Sabbath.

Jonathan Edwards

In the next century, Jonathan Edwards, one of the leading theologians of that era, was equally adamant about the need to keep the Sabbath holy. In the appendix, we have reprinted one of his sermons on the Sabbath, *The Perpetuity and Change of the Sabbath.* In it he said,

> *Therefore, I design now, by the help of God, to show that it is sufficiently revealed in the Scriptures, to be the mind and will of God, that the first day of the week should be distinguished in the Christian church from other days of the week, as a Sabbath, to be devoted to religious exercises.*[13]

His reasoned arguments for why the Sabbath continues and how it has changed should be seriously considered before we decide that the Sabbath was ceremonial law that passed away with Israel.

---

11. Joshua 24:27 "And Joshua said unto all the people, Behold, this stone shall be a witness unto us; for it hath heard all the words of the LORD which he spake unto us: it shall be therefore a witness unto you, lest ye deny your God."
12. Andrew A Bonar, *Letters of Samuel Rutherford* (Edinburgh: Oliphant Anderson & Ferrier, 1891) p. 8
13. *The Works of Jonathan Edwards* (London: William Ball, 34, Paternoster Row,1839) Google Books .Web. October 19th, 2009 vol. 2, p. 94

Nineteenth Century Society

While many theologians in the nineteenth century continued to hold the Reformed position on the Sabbath, we can see the that the whole society considered the Sabbath significant early in the century by looking at the Inaugurations of the Presidents of the United States. On March 4th, 1821, the inauguration fell on the Sabbath. James Monroe, the president-elect, instead of just continuing on with the inauguration, waited until the next day.[14] Zachary Taylor did the same in 1849,[15] and Rutherford B. Hays also waited in 1877.[16] The American government no longer follows this practice.

A wonderful example of one who understood the Sabbath was General Thomas "Stonewall" Jackson, a famous Confederate General in the American Civil War. As he led an army in the field, he understood the sovereignty of God and that victory is not from having more equipment and men.[17] Victory is from the hand of God. As Jonathan said in 1 Samuel 14:6:

> *It may be that the LORD will work for us: for there is no restraint to the LORD to save by many or by few.*[18]

Jackson recognized that the Confederate States of America needed to repent of their sins if they expected God to grant them victory, even though they were greatly outnumbered

---

14. *Inaugural Addresses of the Presidents of the Untied States*, (Bedford, Massachusetts: Applewood Books) *Google Books*. Web. Retrieved November 26th, 2009. vol. 1, p. 43
15. *Ibid*, p. 103
16. *Ibid*, p. 137
17 Psalm 20:7 "Some trust in chariots, and some in horses: but we will remember the name of the LORD our God."
18. 1 Samuel 14:6

by their foes. To that end, he worked to get the Confederate Congress to stop moving the mail on the Sabbath. In regards to that, he said:

> *I believe that God will bless us with success if Christians will but do their duty. For nearly fifteen years Sabbath mails have been, through God's blessing, avoided by me, and I am thankful to say that in no instance has there been an occasion for regret, but, on the contrary, God has made it a source of pure enjoyment for me.*[19]

And again:

> *I do not see how a nation that thus arrays itself, by such a law, against God's holy day can expect to escape his wrath. ... For fifteen years I have refused to mail letters on Sunday or take them out of the office on that day ... I have never sustained a loss in observing what God enjoins ...*[20]

Notice that not only did Jackson speak against the mail being delivered on the Sabbath, he practiced it in his own life. If we want our society to keep the Sabbath, we have to start by keeping it ourselves.

Blue Laws

This view of the Lord's Day continued into the twentieth century. It was normal practice in most of the states in the United States to enforce what were called "Blue Laws." The Blue Laws are those laws that the civil magistrate used to enforce the keeping of the Sabbath. They did not necessarily

---

19. Mary Anna Jackson, *Life and letters of General Thomas J. Jackson* (New York: Harper and Brothers, 1891) p. 76-77
20. *Ibid*, p. 403

require the attendance at church, but they did require the cessation of all business activity. These laws were widely enforced even until the 1980s. Moving into the second half of the twentieth century, many of the states began to repeal their Blue Laws. One of the last ones was Massachusetts, which repealed theirs in 1994.[21] Many states still have laws restricting the sale of alcohol on Sunday, but many of these are not enforced.[22] Even with the modern unconstitutional interpretation of the separation of church and state, the courts have held that it is not the imposition of religion to require a day of rest.[23] The courts have consistently found that the Blue Laws were not a violation of separation of Church and state nor did they restrict the free exercise of religion.[24] Bergan County, New Jersey, is one of the few places in the United States with Blue Laws still in effect.[25] They have found that there is a compelling state interest in forcing a day of rest, because it promotes peace and quiet and improves the productivity of the people.

As the church of Jesus Christ, we need to be asking ourselves if we have maintained the form of sound words that were given to us, or if we have taken our own path. In the

---

21. M.G.L. c. 136, §16. Web. http://www.malegislature.gov/Laws/GeneralLaws/PartI/TitleXX/Chapter136/Section16 Accessed November 4, 2010.

22. Paige Bowers *Will the Recession Doom the Last Sunday Blue Laws?* Time February 22, 2009 Web. Accessed October 20, 2009.

23. Such as McGowan v. Maryland, 366 U.S. 420 (1961), Gallagher v. Crown Kosher Super Market of Massachusetts, Inc., 366 U.S. 617 (1961) and Two Guys from Harrison-Allentown, Inc., v. McGinley, 366 U.S. 582 (1961).

24. "Congress shall make no law respecting an establishment of religion, or prohibiting the free exercise thereof . . ." *United States Constitution*, 1st Amendment.

25. WCB-TV, *Blue Laws Could Get Red Light In Bergen County*, March 13, 2008 Web. http://wcbstv.com/local/blue.laws.bergen.2.676720.html Accessed October 21st, 2009.

past thirty years, our view of the Sabbath has completely changed. This change has not benefited the church, but on the contrary, that period has seen a great increase of worldliness in the church. The Sabbath is a mark that God has given us to set us aside as a sanctified people. When we discard that mark, we end up not looking like a holy people. Instead we look like a hopeless people, because although we profess Christ, we look just like the rest of the world.

CHAPTER 7

The Day

When the Sabbath is discussed, once there is an understanding of the need to keep the Sabbath, the next question we should ask is which day of the week to keep it: the seventh or the first? We could say that Exodus says that we are to keep the Sabbath holy because God created for six days and rested on the seventh. So therefore the seventh day of the week must be the Sabbath. The conclusion could be reached that the church is wrong to keep the Sabbath on Sunday, and that it should really be celebrated on Saturday as the Jews do. There are a few problems with this line of reasoning.

First, we know from the commandments given in scripture that there are two things that are to be remembered when keeping the Sabbath day holy. The first is that God is the creator and the second is that God is the redeemer. When we hold that the day should be the seventh day of the week, we are pointing to every living person's obligation to God as their Creator, but not the obligation of Christians to God as their Redeemer. We have been redeemed. The keeping of the Sabbath day is to be a reminder of our redemption as well.

Israel's Year Reset

When Israel left Egypt to travel to the promised land, God reset their calendar because of His act of redemption. The beginning of the year no longer pointed to creation, instead it was reset to point to their redemption from Egypt. The previous beginning of the year was the autumnal equinox, but the redemption from Egypt changed the calendar to the spring because that was when they were redeemed. God commanded:

> *This month shall be unto you the beginning of months:*
> *it shall be the first month of the year to you.*[1]

This is important to understand, because Israel's redemption from Egypt is a type of the true Israel's redemption from sin, the purchase of the elect from sin through the sacrifice of God's only begotten Son on the cross. By resetting the calendar, God was stating that the second birth of the spirit was more important than the first birth of the flesh. As important as creation was, redemption is more important.

Israel's Sabbath Reset

But it was not just the annual calendar that was to be reset based upon the Passover:

> *Six days shall work be done: but the seventh day is the*
> *sabbath of rest, an holy convocation; ye shall do no*
> *work therein: it is the sabbath of the LORD in all your*
> *dwellings. These are the feasts of the LORD, even holy*

---

1. Exodus 12:2.

72

convocations, which ye shall proclaim in their sea-
sons. In the fourteenth day of the first month at even is
the LORD'S passover. And on the fifteenth day of the
same month is the feast of unleavened bread unto the
LORD: seven days ye must eat unleavened bread. In
the first day ye shall have an holy convocation: ye shall
do no servile work therein. But ye shall offer an offering
made by fire unto the LORD seven days: in the seventh
day is an holy convocation: ye shall do no servile work
therein. [2]

On the fifteenth day of the first month, Abib, God commanded a holy convocation, using the same wording that is used
to command the Sabbath. God is not just resetting the annual calendar based upon the redemption from Egypt, He is
also resetting which day is the seventh day of the week. The
Sabbath previously was every seven days after the start of
creation, but after Israel's redemption from Egypt, every year
the Sabbath is to be reset based on the fifteenth day of the
first month, and all the subsequent Sabbaths in the year were
based on that date. So just as now January 1st is on a different day of the week every year, so was the Israelite Sabbath.

It becomes clearer as the commandment is given for
when to celebrate the Feast of Weeks, also called Pentecost:

And ye shall count unto you from the morrow after
the sabbath, from the day that ye brought the sheaf of
the wave offering; seven sabbaths shall be complete:
Even unto the morrow after the seventh sabbath shall

2. Leviticus 23:3-8.

*ye number fifty days; and ye shall offer a new meat of-
fering unto the LORD.* [3]

The morrow after the Sabbath is when the sheaf offering was
waved. The sheaf offering was commanded to be waved on
the sixteenth of Abib.[4] They were to count seven Sabbaths
after that day, and on the day after the seventh Sabbath there
was to be an offering for the Feast of Weeks, also called the
Feast of the Wheat Harvest.[5] God is not saying that for this
seven week period between Passover and Pentecost,[6] there
was an extra Sabbath day every week. They were not to work
five days and rest on two Sabbaths. In any week, there was
only one Sabbath. The whole Jewish calendar was reset by
the redemption of Egypt, not just the start of the year, but the
start of the week because the Sabbath is to point back to their
redemption from Egypt as stated in Deuteronomy 5.

Israel's Feasts a Picture of History

When we understand the purpose of the Sabbath, that it
is for us to remember that God has redeemed us, then it follows that after the resurrection, the weekly calendar would
be changed but not the annual calendar. The original calendar for the Israelite year was a picture of the history of
the world. The year originally started with the beginning of
the world when it was created, and the first annual feast was
the Passover, also called the Feast of the Unleavened Bread.

---

3   Leviticus 23:15-16.
4. Leviticus 23:11 "And he shall wave the sheaf before the LORD, to be accepted
    for you: on the morrow after the sabbath the priest shall wave it."
5. Exodus 34:22 "And thou shalt observe the feast of weeks, of the firstfruits of
    wheat harvest, and the feast of ingathering at the year's end."
6. Pentecost is a transliteration of the Greek word which means fifty because it
    started on the fiftieth day after the Feast of Unleavened Bread.

The Passover represented God's salvation. The first born of the Israelites being passed over because of the death of the Passover lamb was all a type of the true Passover, when the Lamb of God was killed so that the death we deserve is passed over and laid upon Him. But it was also called the Feast of the Barley Harvest,[7] which was what they used for the wave offering the day after the Passover, to represent Israel being the redeemed people of God.

The next festival on the Israelite calendar was the Feast of the Wheat Harvest, which was also called Pentecost and the Feast of Weeks. The ceremonial aspects of this festival were fulfilled at the day of Pentecost recorded in Acts:

> *And when the day of Pentecost was fully come, they were all with one accord in one place. And suddenly there came a sound from heaven as of a rushing mighty wind, and it filled all the house where they were sitting. And there appeared unto them cloven tongues like as of fire, and it sat upon each of them. And they were all filled with the Holy Ghost, and began to speak with other tongues, as the Spirit gave them utterance.* [8]

The Feast of Weeks in the calendar given by Moses was always to foreshadow that great event, the coming of the Holy Spirit fifty days after the resurrection of Jesus Christ and the gospel going to all nations of the earth. But just as the real Passover came when the Lord Jesus Christ died on the cross,

---

7. Ruth 1:22 "So Naomi returned, and Ruth the Moabitess, her daughter in law, with her, which returned out of the country of Moab: and they came to Bethlehem in the beginning of barley harvest."

8. Acts 2:1-4.

the Feast of Pentecost was always representing the true Pentecost which happened as a moment in history.

The last festival of the year was the Feast of Tabernacles, which was at the end of the year before the Israelites left Egypt. It represents that great harvest at the end of time when we will not be living in this fallen world, but will be rejoicing in heaven - where all things have been made new and the corrupted will be raised in incorruption. Another name for this feast is the Feast of Ingathering:

And the feast of harvest, the firstfruits of thy labours, which thou hast sown in the field: and the feast of ingathering, which is in the end of the year, when thou hast gathered in thy labours out of the field.[9]

This feast represents a time when all of the labor of the church will be gathered out of the field of the world at the end of the age. When the Israelites obeyed and celebrated these feasts, they were proclaiming the whole redemptive plan of God.

Sabbath Points to Christ

For the Israelites, the weekly Sabbath was about pointing to their redemption from Egypt, but for Christians, we should realize that we do not need to point to the type. Even the fact that it would change every year, pointed to the fact that the redemption from the slavery of Egypt was just a picture of a more significant redemption, the redemption that results in eternal life. In 1 Corinthians 10, Paul compares our redemption with the redemption of Israel, because just as Israel was redeemed and baptized in the Red Sea, Christians

---

9. Exodus 23:16.

are redeemed and baptized.[10] The Sabbath changing with the calendar testified to the Israelites that this was just a picture of a reality to come, in the same manner as all of the other events on their calendar.

With our celebration of the Sabbath, we are no longer pointing to the type, instead we point to the antitype, the fulfillment of the type. If we were to change our weekly calendar every year, then we would be testifying that we were not saved by an event that has happened, but we would be testifying to an event that will happen. But since Christ has come, by our celebrating the Lord's Day on the first day of the Roman week, Sunday, the day of Christ's resurrection, we are pointing back to the true resurrection of Christ. Not something that is a physical shadow, but the reality. We were freed from our Egypt, which is enslavement to sin, not just by Jesus' death on the cross. That simply made us a people who were not to experience the wrath of God, but were not free from the bondage of sin. It was the resurrection that makes us free and allows us to not continue to serve sin.

For if we have been planted together in the likeness of his death, we shall be also in the likeness of his resurrection: Knowing this, that our old man is crucified with him, that the body of sin might be destroyed, that henceforth we should not serve sin.[11]

We have hope because of the resurrection. We are passed

---

10   1 Corinthians 10:1-4 "Moreover, brethren, I would not that ye should be igno-
      rant, how that all our fathers were under the cloud, and all passed through the
      sea; And were all baptized unto Moses in the cloud and in the sea; And did all
      eat the same spiritual meat; And did all drink the same spiritual drink: for they
      drank of that spiritual Rock that followed them: and that Rock was Christ."
11.   Romans 6:5-6.

over from the eternal punishment not because of the cru-
cifixion, but because of the resurrection, we become the
people of promise. We are the people who have left Egypt.
The weekly Sabbath was changed to be a declaration of that,
which is why the celebration of the Lord's Supper is directly
connected to the Sabbath:

> *When ye come together therefore into one place, this is
> not to eat the Lord's supper.* [12]

The primary purpose of the gathering together on the Lord's
Day is to worship God and remember that He saved us. That
is why the Lord's Supper should be part of the worship service, because the day is about proclaiming the death and resurrection of Jesus Christ, and through the breaking of bread
we are to declare it until He comes.[13] We are to celebrate the
Christian Sabbath on the first day of the week.

The Example of the Early Church

Another reason we know that the Sabbath has changed
from the seventh to the first day of the week is the example
of the early church. There are several examples in the New
Testament of Christians meeting together on the Lord's Day
to worship. For example:

> *And upon the first day of the week, when the disciples
> came together to break bread, Paul preached unto
> them, ready to depart on the morrow; and continued
> his speech until midnight.* [14]

---

12. 1 Corinthians 11:20.
13. 1 Corinthians 11:26 "For as often as ye eat this bread, and drink this cup, ye do
    shew the Lord's death till he come."
14. Acts 20:7.

And

> *Upon the first day of the week let every one of you lay by him in store, as God hath prospered him, that there be no gatherings when I come.* [15]

The Bible also clearly says that Jesus rose from the dead on the first day:

> *In the end of the sabbath, as it began to dawn toward the first day of the week, came Mary Magdalene and the other Mary to see the sepulchre.* [16]

A Full Day

Another way our churches have corrupted the Sabbath is in the view of what a day is. God is clear that the week is divided into seven days. Each day covers twenty-four hours. But how many people in our churches who profess that Sunday is a day for rest and worship, actually believe that only an hour or two are for rest and worship? The rest of the day is to seek their own pleasure. Many would like to think that when God said we are to work six days and on the seventh we are to rest, that He really meant we are only to worship for a couple hours in the morning and then spend the rest of the time doing whatever seems right in our own eyes. But most of us recognize that the six days for work require most of the time in those days to be spent in labor. We rob from God when we shorten the Sabbath. We are like the people that Amos writes about:

> *Saying, When will the new moon be gone, that we*

---

15. 1 Corinthians 16:2.
16. Matthew 28:1.

may sell corn? and the sabbath, that we may set forth
wheat, making the ephah small, and the shekel great,
and falsifying the balances by deceit? [17]

God has given us a great blessing in the Sabbath and instead
of rejoicing in the gift, we say like the people of Amos' time,
"When will these times that God gave us to rejoice in be over
so we can seek after the things of the earth." God equates
these people to those who cheat and steal from the poor.

Several verses later, God swears that He will never forget. When we take the gift of the Sabbath and treat it as
chains rather than a balm to our souls, we should expect
the punishment of God because we are acting as though
we worship this world. When we shorten the Sabbath from
the twenty-four hours that God has blessed us with and ex-
change it for two, we are despising the things of God and if
we are His sons, we should expect His chastisement.

When we think of a day, we need to reset our thinking
about it based upon the Word of God. In our calendar, we
define a day to be from midnight to midnight. But in reality,
if we stay up past midnight, we usually do not say that we
have been up for two days. We normally consider our day
is ended after a period of sleep. But biblically, a day is well
defined:

And God called the light Day, and the darkness he
called Night. And the evening and the morning were
the first day. [18]

Our definition that a day starts at midnight is rather

---

17. Amos 8:5.
18. Genesis 1:5.

nonsensical. Until clocks were in wide use, which in many parts of the world they are still not, it was impossible to know when a day started. But since the day was defined around man, it was, of course, ambiguous. God's plan, however, is that we are to know when a day begins:

And God said, Let there be lights in the firmament of the heaven to divide the day from the night; and let them be for signs, and for seasons, and for days, and years[19]

According to the Bible, when the sun goes down, that is the beginning of the next day. In Genesis 1 it says "And the evening and the morning were the first day." The day begins in the evening when the sun goes down and continues through the night and morning until the next evening. We can debate about what minute exactly that day starts. Israelite rabbis determined that it starts when it is dark enough to see three stars in the sky.[20] That is not necessarily correct, but the main point is that it is easily knowable. It is not an arbitrary point that was set by mankind getting together and agreeing on it, it was set by the decree of God.

The impact of understanding what the Sabbath day is is important to your life. God does not want you to spend Saturday evening pursuing your own pleasures or even doing good work, and then Sunday morning be tired and unfit for worship. God's plan is that you start preparing for worship on Saturday night through private and family devotions. The gathering of God's people is not to be the start of the

19. Genesis 1:14.
20. Joseph Barclay. *The Talmud* (London: John Murray, Albemarle Street, 1878) Retrieved from Google Books. Web. November 4th, 2009. p. 86, note.

time of worship on the Sabbath, it is to be in the middle of it. After you have sought God alone, and after you have put aside the distractions from work and other activities to focus on God, then God's people gather on Sunday morning. They worship God together after they have prepared their minds and hearts, having already started their worship before they gather with others.

The Sabbath as a Gift

God has given His people a great gift in the Sabbath day. The gift of a day, a twenty-four hour day, to put aside the things that we have to bear on a daily basis and remember the world is not about those burdens. Those burdens are given to us by our Father in heaven to disciple us and conform us to the image of His only begotten Son. It is a day to remember the God who has freed us from our enslavement to sin, that while we still struggle against the flesh, we can have victory over sin. The Sabbath is a day to remember that Jesus Christ was nailed to the cross for our sin. How can we not want to celebrate that entire day?

CHAPTER 8

The Rest

When we consider the Sabbath, it is easy for us to become like the Pharisees. The Pharisees attacked Jesus for breaking the Sabbath. Since they trusted in their own righteousness, this is somewhat understandable. They were well aware of the destruction of Jerusalem due to their ancestors ignoring the Sabbath in the past. In many ways, they continued to break the Sabbath, because there is no record of them giving the land its Sabbath rest or restoring the tribes to their inheritances, which are commandments regarding the Sabbath and Jubilee years. But in some ways, they also became very serious about keeping the Sabbath. They added to the biblical Sabbath laws with their own sense of righteousness. Consider from John:

> *Jesus saith unto him, Rise, take up thy bed, and walk. And immediately the man was made whole, and took up his bed, and walked: and on the same day was the sabbath. The Jews therefore said unto him that was cured, It is the sabbath day: it is not lawful for thee to carry thy bed.* [1]

---

1.   John 5:8-10.

Clearly, taking up his bed and walking was not work according to the proper interpretation of the law. Otherwise Jesus would be leading his neighbor into sin,[2] which itself is a sin and we know there was no sin in Him. When we consider what we should do on the Sabbath, we need to make certain that we have a biblical definition of rest, unlike the Pharisees.

God's Work on the Sabbath

To understand what rest is we need to consider what is revealed about God's rest. The first giving of the Sabbath commandment focuses on how the Sabbath is based upon the creation order. We know that on the seventh day God rested after creating the heavens and the earth. After the Pharisees sought to slay Jesus because He told the man to carry his bed, Jesus responded by defending himself from creation:

> But Jesus answered them, My Father worketh hitherto, and I work. [3]

Even when God rested, He still worked. He worked by upholding the world, as it says in Hebrews 1:3 that Christ was "... upholding all things by the word of his power, when he had by himself purged our sins, sat down on the right hand of the Majesty on high:" It is important for us to understand what work we should continue to do on the Sabbath and what should be put aside. Scripture does define it, but it is difficult for us to understand it. Part of having a proper view of the Sabbath is to understand God's mercy in giving it to us and

---

2. Leviticus 19:17 "Thou shalt not hate thy brother in thine heart: thou shalt in any wise rebuke thy neighbour, and not suffer sin upon him."
3. John 5:17.

not trying to push the limits on how much work we can do, instead of rejoicing in God's kindness.

Rest Defined by the Law

There are some passages that direct us to some boundaries about what is proper to do on the Sabbath. The Jewish Rabbis added many laws in the Talmud to define exactly what was forbidden and allowed. For example, it was forbidden to place an egg on the sand because it might roast.[4] Another example the Pharisees came up with the concept of a Sabbath day's journey.[5] The length of what the Pharisees said was acceptable to walk on the Sabbath probably came from Numbers 35:

And the cities shall they have to dwell in; and the suburbs of them shall be for their cattle, and for their goods, and for all their beasts. And the suburbs of the cities, which ye shall give unto the Levites, shall reach from the wall of the city and outward a thousand cubits round about. And ye shall measure from without the city on the east side two thousand cubits, and on the south side two thousand cubits, and on the west side two thousand cubits, and on the north side two thousand cubits; and the city shall be in the midst: this shall be to them the suburbs of the cities. [6]

Notice in these two verses that the distances are different. The first distance specified is one thousand cubits and the

4. Joseph Barclay. *The Talmud* (London: John Murray, Albemarle Street, 1878) Retrieved from Google Books. Web. November 4th, 2009. p. 87
5. Acts 1:12 "Then returned they unto Jerusalem from the mount called Olivet, which is from Jerusalem a sabbath day's journey."
6. Numbers 35:3-5..

second is two thousand cubits. The thousand cubits is the distance that they were allowed to build their barns for their animals, but the actual land that they had use of was an additional thousand cubits for grazing and harvesting. The distance of a Sabbath day's journey is two thousand cubits, because they would have to feed, water and milk their animals so they would not be cruel to them, even on the Sabbath. The Pharisees understood that the works of necessity needed to be continued on the Sabbath day, so they allowed a walk out to their barns and back. The problem is that nowhere in the Bible does it say how far you are allowed to walk on the Sabbath. Jesus spoke of the works of necessity you are allowed to do on the Sabbath:

> *"And he said unto them, What man shall there be among you, that shall have one sheep, and if it fall into a pit on the sabbath day, will he not lay hold on it, and lift it out?"*[7]

The Sabbath was made for man and not man for the Sabbath. When we start to say that the Sabbath prevents us from doing things that it is obvious we need to do, we are changing what God gave for our good into a curse.

Works of Necessity

The works of necessity should be considered those things that could not be done the day before. In scripture, the day before the Sabbath is referred to as the Preparation Day.[8] We need to understand that what we can do beforehand we

---

7. Matthew 12:11.

8 Matthew 27:62 "Now the next day, that followed the day of the preparation, the chief priests and Pharisees came together unto Pilate,"

should, but there are certainly things that cannot be done before that need to be done on the Sabbath. After all, the Sabbath was a feast day[9] and serving a feast does involve work, and that obviously is not contrary to the word of God. To understand where God draws the line on what is a work of necessity, we should consider some examples from scripture.

One example we should consider is the commandments regarding the gathering of manna:

And it came to pass, that on the sixth day they gathered twice as much bread, two omers for one man: and all the rulers of the congregation came and told Moses. And he said unto them, This is that which the LORD hath said, Tomorrow is the rest of the holy sabbath unto the LORD: bake that which ye will bake to day, and seethe that ye will seethe; and that which remaineth over lay up for you to be kept until the morning. And they laid it up till the morning, as Moses bade: and it did not stink, neither was there any worm therein. And Moses said, Eat that to day; for to day is a sabbath unto the LORD: to day ye shall not find it in the field. Six days ye shall gather it; but on the seventh day, which is the sabbath, in it there shall be none. [10]

When God was providing directly for His people through manna from heaven, there was no necessity to gather on the seventh day. We do not have to work on the Sabbath to provide for our families. When we think we do, we need to understand that we are saying it is not God who provides for

---

9. Hosea 2:11 "I will also cause all her mirth to cease, her feast days, her new moons, and her sabbaths, and all her solemn feasts."
10. Exodus 16:22-26.

87

us. We are rejecting what the Lord taught us to pray, "Give us this day our daily bread." We are saying that it used to be God that gave us our food, but now it is the work of our own hands. God is still the only one that gives an increase. The labor is ours to do, but it is God that gives us the increase and allows us to reap from that sowing. God has specifically said that the Sabbath day is not for working to feed our families. When we think that we can increase our prosperity by going against God's commandments, we should not be surprised when that productivity breeds worms and stinks. Not literally, but we should not expect for that work to be blessed any more than the disobedience to God in the desert by trying to keep the manna overnight.

Related to what is permissible to do on the Sabbath, Jesus did not rebuke His disciples when they plucked enough grain for their personal consumption:

> *And it came to pass on the second sabbath after the first, that he went through the corn fields; and his disciples plucked the ears of corn, and did eat, rubbing them in their hands.*[11]

So if we take the definition of work too far the other way, we become too restrictive. To do some food preparation on the Sabbath day is clearly acceptable in the sight of God, but there are limits.

Boundaries

Another commandment from Moses to consider:

---

11. Luke 6:1.

Ye shall kindle no fire throughout your habitations upon the sabbath day.[12]

We could say that God is saying that they are to have no fire burning on the Sabbath day in their houses. But God is not cruel, there are times when it gets quite cold in Israel. For them to not have fires in their habitations would make the Sabbath day a day of suffering rather than delight. It is important to read what the commandment actually says. What it says is not to kindle a fire in your house on the Sabbath day. Before the advent of matches, kindling a fire took a great deal of work. That work was to be done the day before, but to add wood to a fire to heat your habitation is not against God's law, just the kindling of the fire. Some other related verses:

And while the children of Israel were in the wilderness, they found a man that gathered sticks upon the sabbath day. And they that found him gathering sticks brought him unto Moses and Aaron, and unto all the congregation. And they put him in ward, because it was not declared what should be done to him. And the LORD said unto Moses, The man shall be surely put to death: all the congregation shall stone him with stones without the camp.[13]

If a man was out gathering sticks on the Sabbath day that was clearly against the law, because that was something he could have done on the Preparation Day. His slothfulness does not then make it acceptable behavior. We need to seriously consider how we treat the Preparation Day. There are

12. Exodus 35:3.
13. Numbers 15:32-35.

times when we have to suffer because of our previous sin. Just because this man sinned and did not prepare the day before did not mean that he was allowed to break the Sabbath. We need to consider whether we really prepared for a day of worship and rest and have done all that we can to eliminate things that will distract us from spending that day with God.

Today's Works of Necessity

The works of necessity that can be done on the Sabbath could change with different societies. If today no one worked at power plants on the Sabbath, that would make the day a curse and not a blessing. People in our age are not accustomed to living without the benefits of electricity, including temperature control, nor are our houses designed to minimize the discomfort of an environment without electricity. If we say that there were cultures which previously existed without electricity so it is not necessary for our society, we ignore the reality of our time. In our society, there are people whose lives are significantly lengthened through the use of devices that require electricity, and if we say that all of those should just be cut off, it is not to give us a day of rest for our good, but would actually cause great harm and death.[14] Of course, the power companies have a responsibility to move as much work as possible to other days to minimize their staff requirements on the Sabbath.

Other work that needs to be done on the Sabbath would include positions such as police officers. We all desire to live in a country where constant patrols are not needed, but we do not. We even see with Nehemiah, when he was concerned

---

14. For example respirators, dialysis machines, etc.

about the judgment of God falling on Israel again for breaking the Sabbath, he has people work on the Sabbath:

> *Did not your fathers thus, and did not our God bring*
> *all this evil upon us, and upon this city? yet ye bring*
> *more wrath upon Israel by profaning the sabbath. And*
> *it came to pass, that when the gates of Jerusalem be-*
> *gan to be dark before the sabbath, I commanded that*
> *the gates should be shut, and charged that they should*
> *not be opened till after the sabbath: and some of my*
> *servants set I at the gates, that there should no burden*
> *be brought in on the sabbath day.* [15]

Nehemiah sees the evil that is being done, buying and selling
on the Sabbath, and his response is to command his servants
to work on the Sabbath. It would be easy for us to look at
that situation and say he was breaking the Sabbath to assure
the keeping of the Sabbath, but this is the civil magistrate
fulfilling his responsibility by fearing God and constraining
the evil in the community. It is not breaking the Sabbath,
but doing a necessary work that for obvious reasons could
not be done on a different day. It is interesting that after
enforcing the law for a few Sabbaths and Nehemiah threat-
ening to lay hands on the merchants for continuing to try to
buy and sell on the Sabbath, he then assigns the task to the
Levites to continue to maintain the watch on the walls.[16] As
the civil magistrate, it is reasonable that his servants would
have the responsibility. But as soon as the situation is under

---

15. Nehemiah 13:18-19.
16. Nehemiah 13:22 "And I commanded the Levites that they should cleanse them-
    selves, and that they should come and keep the gates, to sanctify the sabbath
    day. Remember me, O my God, concerning this also, and spare me according to
    the greatness of thy mercy."

control, the responsibility is transferred to the priesthood, whom God has already given responsibilities on the Sabbath.

The Priest's Work

Another example of work that God clearly condones, and Jesus Christ even reiterates the commandment regarding it, is the priestly work that is to take place on the Sabbath. When the Jews are desiring to kill Jesus Christ because they thought He had broken the Sabbath:

> Jesus answered and said unto them, I have done one work, and ye all marvel. Moses therefore gave unto you circumcision; (not because it is of Moses, but of the fathers;) and ye on the sabbath day circumcise a man. If a man on the sabbath day receive circumcision, that the law of Moses should not be broken; are ye angry at me, because I have made a man every whit whole on the sabbath day?[17]

Jesus was pointing out that the priests understood that there was some work they were to do regardless of whether it was the Sabbath. God said that a male child was to be circumcised on the eighth day, even if it was the Sabbath. God also commanded the priests to make certain sacrifices every Sabbath:

> And on the sabbath day two lambs of the first year without spot, and two tenth deals of flour for a meat offering, mingled with oil, and the drink offering thereof: This is the burnt offering of every sabbath, beside the continual burnt offering, and his drink offering. [18]

---

17. John 7:21-23.
18. Numbers 28:9-10.

It took work for the Levites to prepare these offerings and to offer them, but God made it clear they were to offer them every Sabbath day.

Travel on the Sabbath

Another profession that must be continued on the Sabbath would be hospitality. Obviously, our current system where we have removed hospitality from the home to businesses such as hotels is not biblical, but it is clear that it was not a sin to travel even for long periods of time.

> Go to now, ye that say, Today or tomorrow we will go into such a city, and continue there a year, and buy and sell, and get gain:[19]

While this passage is about the sovereignty of God, it uses the example of traveling and staying in a city away from your home. This implies that there is a place for you to stay and live, and that people providing these services do not stop on the Sabbath. When we consider what it means to rest, we need to carefully examine how God defines rest.

Buying and Selling

There are other things, however, that the scripture clearly restricts from being done on the Sabbath. The Sabbath is explicitly not for buying and selling. God has given us a day that we are to rest so that we recognize that God is our provider. When the people of Judah returned to the land after the Babylonian captivity, this was one of the things that they covenanted together to stop.

> And if the people of the land bring ware or any victuals

---

19. James 4:13.

on the sabbath day to sell, that we would not buy it of them on the sabbath, or on the holy day: and that we would leave the seventh year, and the exaction of every debt.[20]

God has made it clear that whether we are buying something to provide for ourselves or if we are selling something to provide a profit to ourselves, it is not to be done on the Sabbath day. God wants a constant reminder in our schedules that He is the provider and not us. The modern practice of having coffee shops and restaurants in churches so that people can have their needs filled is returning to practices similar to the ones that Jesus rebuked by flipping over the tables in the temple. God's house is not to be a house of merchandise[21] and God's day is not to be a day for merchandising either.

God gives us a clear warning of what people that desire to do business on the Sabbath are like:

Saying, When will the new moon be gone, that we may sell corn? and the sabbath, that we may set forth wheat, making the ephah small, and the shekel great, and falsifying the balances by deceit? That we may buy the poor for silver, and the needy for a pair of shoes; yea, and sell the refuse of the wheat?[22]

The people who desire to shorten the time that God calls us to focus on Him are the same kind of people that rob the poor, sell shoddy goods, steal through unjust weights and delight in taking advantage of people. This is how God

---

20. Nehemiah 10:31.
21. John 2:16 "And said unto them that sold doves, Take these things hence; make not my Father's house an house of merchandise."
22. Amos 8:5-6.

describes those who desire for the Sabbath to be over so that they can participate in those activities. How much worse are those who do not suspend the buying and selling at all on the Sabbath, and profess to be the children of God? We live in a culture where some restaurants have their busiest times on Sunday afternoon after the church services end. That is an abomination in God's sight and we who are in the church must repent, if we desire God to remove His curse from us. God has given us a day to rest from our labors, but instead we desire the yoke of providing for ourselves to lie heavier upon our shoulders and on the shoulders of those we buy from on the Sabbath.

Cry Out for Mercy

When we consider the things that we should do and should not do on the Sabbath, we need to understand as Nehemiah did that all of these things are not perfectly clear. God did not just write out in detail what we could and could not do. He desires for us to meditate and search the scriptures to find His will for everything. He commands us to fear Him and grow in our knowledge of Him so that we do the things that He has commanded for our good. When we consider what we do on the Sabbath, we need to understand that we will fall short in our understanding and we need to cry out with Nehemiah:

> *Remember me, O my God, concerning this also, and spare me according to the greatness of thy mercy.*[23]

---

23. Nehemiah 13:22.

95

CHAPTER 9

The Mercy

Mercy is directly tied to the Sabbath, therefore it is hard to see why any Christian delights in disregarding it. God shows His mercy to us by giving us a day to worship and rest from our labors, instead of constantly toiling in our work. The people in the world think that they need to work every day to provide for themselves, while we recognize that all provision comes from God. But we also need to recognize what our duty is toward God:

> *I beseech you therefore, brethren, by the mercies of God, that you present your bodies a living sacrifice, holy, acceptable to God, which is your reasonable service.* [1]

We do not have any time that we can rightly call our own. When God opens our eyes so that we can see His gift of salvation through his mercy and grace, our only legitimate response is to be constantly doing His will. We are a *"slave of righteousness"* and God has the right to command us to be about His work every minute. But He is not a cruel taskmaster; instead, He gives us many good gifts. He gives us sleep.

---

1. Romans 12:1.

He gives us times of celebration. Another of those gifts is the Sabbath. The Sabbath should be a constant testimony to the mercy of God in giving us a time to rest from our work.

God's Kindness to Us

It is easy for us to turn that picture of mercy into a picture of mourning. God will not allow us to work all seven days. When our employer gives us a day off, we are thankful, but when our Creator gives us a day off from the burdens of this world, our response is to say, "How cruel." We need to stop being hypocrites in our thinking. When God gives us fifty-two days in a year off from work, we need to acknowledge that it is His kindness as well.

The Pharisees wanted to put Jesus to death because they could not understand this concept. When Christ's disciples were picking grain and eating it on the Sabbath, the Pharisees asked Jesus, "Why do they on the sabbath day that which is not lawful?"[2] The Pharisees thought that the Sabbath was about God punishing men. They were like the man in the parable who hid the one talent he was given in the ground, and when the lord came to reckon with his servants:

Then he which had received the one talent came and said, Lord, I knew thee that thou art an hard man, reaping where thou hast not sown, and gathering where thou hast not strawed: And I was afraid, and went and hid thy talent in the earth: lo, there thou hast that is thine. His lord answered and said unto him, Thou wicked and slothful servant, thou knewest that I reap where I sowed not, and gather where I have not

---

2. Mark 2:27.

strawed: Thou oughtest therefore to have put my money to the exchangers, and then at my coming I should have received mine own with usury. Take therefore the talent from him, and give it unto him which hath ten talents. For unto every one that hath shall be given, and he shall have abundance: but from him that hath not shall be taken away even that which he hath. And cast ye the unprofitable servant into outer darkness: there shall be weeping and gnashing of teeth.[3]

We need to recognize how we are blaspheming the name of God when we say God is restrictive and harsh, because He tells us to take a day of rest. We are the servant who says that God is demanding of us things when He has no right. If we really believed that was the character of God, what would the other six days of our week look like? Every minute of our time should be consumed with doing the work of God. Whenever we have a moment of relaxation, we are testifying that we do not believe that God is a cruel taskmaster, just as that servant did by burying the talent in the ground. If he truly thought the lord was as he described him, he would have put the talent out at least to the moneychangers. If we truly thought that God intended to punish us by restricting the activities that we are to do on a day, then would we not act much differently the rest of the time?

Instead of being like the Pharisees, we need to understand Jesus' response to them.

And he said unto them, The sabbath was made for

---

3. Matthew 25:24-30.

*man, and not man for the sabbath: Therefore the Son
of man is Lord also of the sabbath.* [4]

Those who want to get rid of the Sabbath do not understand
that the Sabbath is a testimony to the mercy of God. God
made the Sabbath as a gift to man for our good. When we
take it and make it about what we are not allowed to do, we
are forgetting that God is the perfect Father who loves His
children as only a father can and will not give them what is
evil.[5] Instead, He gives only good gifts to His children, and
the Sabbath is one of those good gifts.

Acts of Mercy

Since Jesus Christ is Lord of the Sabbath, we can understand how the commandments that were given regarding
acts of mercy are perfectly appropriate on the Sabbath. We
should see the Sabbath as an act of mercy to us, so therefore we are to go and do acts of mercy to others. It reflects
the character of the one who bought and redeemed us. The
reaction of the Pharisees when Jesus healed on the Sabbath
was to consider that they needed to obey verses such as this:

*Six days may work be done; but in the seventh is the
sabbath of rest, holy to the LORD: whosoever doeth
any work in the sabbath day, he shall surely be put to
death.*[6]

However, they did not consider that even when He commanded that they were not to work on the Sabbath, He also

---

4. Mark 2:27-28.
5. Matthew 7:11 "If ye then, being evil, know how to give good gifts unto your
    children, how much more shall your Father which is in heaven give good things
    to them that ask him?"
6. Exodus 31:15.

insisted that they show love to their neighbor. When we interpret any of God's laws as a curse to us rather than a blessing, we are ignoring the fact that God says all of His laws are summed up in loving your neighbor as yourself.[7] We take a law and make it say something that God never intended it to say, specifically that you cannot aid your neighbor in his distress, so that Jesus said:

> But if ye had known what this meaneth, I will have mercy, and not sacrifice, ye would not have condemned the guiltless.[8]

When we say that an act of mercy and kindness is not allowed on the Sabbath, we are thinking about God as the Pharisees thought about God. God showed mercy to us by giving us the Sabbath and we are to respond by showing mercy to others. When we say the Sabbath stops our obligation to show love to those around us, we change the blessing that God gives us through the Sabbath into a curse:

> Bring no more vain oblations; incense is an abomination unto me; the new moons and sabbaths, the calling of assemblies, I cannot away with; it is iniquity, even the solemn meeting. Your new moons and your appointed feasts my soul hateth: they are a trouble unto me; I am weary to bear them. [9]

When we turn the Sabbath from a day of mercy to a day of

---

7. Romans 13:9 "For this, Thou shalt not commit adultery, Thou shalt not kill, Thou shalt not steal, Thou shalt not bear false witness, Thou shalt not covet; and if there be any other commandment, it is briefly comprehended in this saying, namely, Thou shalt love thy neighbour as thyself."

8   Matthew 12:7.

9   Isaiah 1:13-14.

obligation, we change it from something that God delights in and make it something that is offensive to Him.

The Pharisees' Fear of God

With that context, we need to remember that this was one of the driving factors for the scribes and the Pharisees to decide they needed to put Jesus to death.[10] On one hand, it is somewhat understandable. Their nation had been dispersed from the land for seventy years because their forefathers had ignored the Sabbath. They were operating from a sense of the fear of God. They feared the destruction of God, but they did not fear God as a Father who loves them. They feared God as a pagan fears the god he believes in, as one who never knows what is going to cause that god to send forth his punishment. Their sacrifices are to appease the false god's thirst for blood. That is not how we are to view the true God. We do not have a god that is like a drunkard in heaven, leaving us to wonder what we might say or do to set him off into a rampage. He is a good Father that has told His children what to do and when they fail to do it, like a good father, he chastens them, not arbitrarily, but deliberately.[11]

When the Pharisees accused Jesus of healing on the Sabbath, it was truly a testimony that they did not know God:

And, behold, there was a man which had his hand

---

10. John 5:18 "Therefore the Jews sought the more to kill him, because he not only had broken the sabbath, but said also that God was his Father, making himself equal with God."

11. Hebrews 12:5-7 "And ye have forgotten the exhortation which speaketh unto you as unto children, My son, despise not thou the chastening of the Lord, nor faint when thou art rebuked of him: For whom the Lord loveth he chasteneth, and scourgeth every son whom he receiveth. If ye endure chastening, God dealeth with you as with sons; for what son is he whom the father chasteneth not?"

withered. And they asked him, saying, Is it lawful to heal on the sabbath days? that they might accuse him. And he said unto them, What man shall there be among you, that shall have one sheep, and if it fall into a pit on the sabbath day, will he not lay hold on it, and lift it out? How much then is a man better than a sheep? Wherefore it is lawful to do well on the sabbath days. Then saith he to the man, Stretch forth thine hand. And he stretched it forth; and it was restored whole, like as the other. Then the Pharisees went out, and held a council against him, how they might destroy him. [12]

When they asked the question of whether it was lawful to heal on the Sabbath day, they should have understood that since there were regular chores that they had to do on the Sabbath, emergencies could happen on the Sabbath that they dealt with, and circumcisions were commanded to be performed on the Sabbath, they could show other forms of mercy on the Sabbath. When God allows them to handle all of the normal actions that show mercy, how could He not to a greater extent say that we should do the same for men?

Showing God's Mercy

When we consider how this applies today, the church tends to make the worship service more focused on how to give the people an emotional high than glorifying God. We move people through singing praises to God, eloquent preaching of the word or rejoicing in being with the people

---

12. Matthew 12:10-14.

of God. Those things are good things, but in that mix, we must also remember that:

> *Pure religion and undefiled before God and the Father is this, To visit the fatherless and widows in their affliction, and to keep himself unspotted from the world.*[13]

When we make the Sabbath to be solely about resting from our labors, and not also about practicing pure and undefiled religion, we are acting like the Pharisees rather than Christ. Time after time, Jesus Christ healed on the Sabbath day. This antagonized the Jews, but Christ was more interested in showing the perpetual mercy of God. Do we show the same mercy of God to the communities around us, not just by not making them work on the Sabbath, but also by using the time on the Sabbath to show the mercy of God?

---

13. James 1:27.

CHAPTER 10

The Delight

The purpose of the Sabbath day is to have a taste of heaven on earth. In heaven, we will know in full. Teaching and edifying of the saints will stop, because we will know as we are now known.[1] Prophecy will also pass away. We will not need a teacher because we will have been made one with Christ in the same sense that a bride is made one with her husband. That is what the focus of the Sabbath day should be: rejoicing in our time with our husband and choosing to do just those things that He has commanded us. The goal is for it to be like heaven. The picture will never be perfect, but if we are not pointing to the goal, we are failing in what our worship service should be about. It should be about rejoicing because we are with the body of Christ and because we are in His presence. It is a testimony to the world that our focus is on the better country.

Desire to Spend Time With God

We need to ask ourselves, why would the church ever not want to keep the Sabbath? God has set aside a day for us to seek to grow closer to Him. This is a day to delight in the

---

1. Hebrews 8:11.

ways of God. It is a day where we do not have the stresses and difficulties that we should be dealing with on a daily basis if we are doing the work of the Lord. Why would the church not delight that God has set apart a day for us every week? Why do we kick against the goads? Is it not because we do not want to be told what to do? We are like a small child at bedtime who is told to go to bed and argues and resists even though he needs the rest. That is the nature of our sinful flesh. In our flesh, we never want to do what God says is good. We are fools from the beginning and only through faith can we walk with wisdom. We can then delight in those things that God has commanded for our good always.

When we do not delight in the Sabbath, we should consider it from the perspective of Jesus Christ:

> *In whom ye also trusted, after that ye heard the word of truth, the gospel of your salvation: in whom also after that ye believed, ye were sealed with that holy Spirit of promise, Which is the earnest of our inheritance until the redemption of the purchased possession, unto the praise of his glory.* [2]

We have a promise from Him that he will come and redeem us in the Holy Spirit. We are the people who because of our disobedience are slaves to sin, so Jesus Christ died on the cross to purchase our freedom. He then takes us and makes us His bride. Our husband, who rescued us from eternal damnation, asks us to spend the day with Him and we say that we do not want to. Consider if a man asked his wife to spend the day with him and not to do anything but to focus

---

2. Ephesians 1:13-14.

on improving their marriage, if that wife spent the whole time saying that she really did not want to be there, that she wished it was only for two hours rather than a whole day, and she asked what they were going to do because she really did not want to spend time with him unless they were really going to do something that she found fun. How would the husband feel? Would he feel that his wife cared for him? Would he feel that his bride wanted to be married to him? When we try to avoid the clear scriptural commandments about the Sabbath, that is how we are treating God.

God understands this reaction, because it has happened before, when Israel played the harlot by following false gods:

Plead with your mother, plead: for she is not my wife, neither am I her husband: let her therefore put away her whoredoms out of her sight, and her adulteries from between her breasts; Lest I strip her naked, and set her as in the day that she was born, and make her as a wilderness, and set her like a dry land, and slay her with thirst. And I will not have mercy upon her children; for they be the children of whoredoms. For their mother hath played the harlot: she that conceived them hath done shamefully: for she said, I will go after my lovers, that give me my bread and my water, my wool and my flax, mine oil and my drink. Therefore, behold, I will hedge up thy way with thorns, and make a wall, that she shall not find her paths. And she shall follow after her lovers, but she shall not overtake them; and she shall seek them, but shall not find them: then shall she say, I will go and return to my first husband; for then was it better with me than now. For she did

SANCTIFIED BY GOD

not know that I gave her corn, and wine, and oil, and multiplied her silver and gold, which they prepared for Baal. Therefore will I return, and take away my corn in the time thereof, and my wine in the season thereof, and will recover my wool and my flax given to cover her nakedness. And now will I discover her lewdness in the sight of her lovers, and none shall deliver her out of mine hand. I will also cause all her mirth to cease, her feast days, her new moons, and her sabbaths, and all her solemn feasts.[3]

Because Israel chased after other gods and false worship, God declared that He is not her husband and that the punishment for that is to take away her Sabbaths. Because it is the scriptural metaphor that is being used, it is valid to think of this in terms of a human husband and wife. The husband says, "I want to spend time with you when you come to where I set my name. I want us to rejoice together;" and the wife decides to chase other men. At some point in time, as patient as that husband may be, he is going to say, "I am not going to set aside time for us to be together." When Israel commits adultery against God, God punishes them by removing the scheduled times together, because she was no longer acting like his bride.

American Church's Delight in God

When we consider this in the light of most churches in America and the nation as a whole, we were a nation that kept the Sabbath until the last hundred years. We were a nation that delighted in our time with God, but now we

---

3. Hosea 2:2-11,

108

delight in chasing the idols of our age. Hasn't God removed His Sabbath from us? Is He not now treating us as a group of people who are not His bride? The bride delights in the bridegroom, and we need to understand just how apostate the church is when we do not desire to be with our husband, especially considering where we are in the courtship process. We are in the betrothal period, the time between engagement and marriage. While Jesus Christ is with the Father preparing a place for His bride and a feast for the celebration of the wedding of all weddings, we do not even want to spend time with Him. It should frighten us that the church does not desire to be with the groom. It should be even more frightening if we personally do not desire to spend the day with the one we say we love.

Delight in Heaven

When we do not want to delight in the Sabbath, we also need to understand that we are saying that we will not delight in heaven. Heaven is about spending time with God:

> *And the city had no need of the sun, neither of the moon, to shine in it: for the glory of God did lighten it, and the Lamb is the light thereof.*[4]

Because God's glory is in heaven, the radiance of His glory is sufficient for all light. All those with a heavenly inheritance when they die will go to be with Christ. We can say those words, but do we truly believe that it is better to be with Christ than to be with the things of this world? If we do, then why do we not delight in the time that God has given us to spend with Him? We should not despise such a

---

4.   Revelation 21:23,

precious gift. We just need to understand that when we do not delight in the gift of the Sabbath, it reflects our attitude toward the Giver.

Consider the things that will take place in heaven, in addition to being in God's presence. In His presence, our response will be the same as John, Paul, Isaiah and the angels: to worship. We read that heaven is filled with singing, singing about the holiness of God, about the mercy of God in redeeming us, and about the death of Christ and the worthiness of God.[5] In heaven, our focus will be on being servants of God rather than providing for ourselves. All of these things should be our focus on the Sabbath. Even the Lord's Supper points to us drinking the cup with Him in heaven. The commandment to keep the Sabbath is to point us to an earthly delight which is to be a foretaste of heaven.

Revival of the Church

We talk about how we wish there was a revival in the church. We wish for the church of the twenty-first century to evangelize better, to edify the saints better and to be impacting the community more for God's glory. In this country during the seventeenth and eighteenth centuries, the church was much more effective in doing those things, but now it is not. We need to be about the business of restoring these things as Isaiah says:

And they that shall be of thee shall build the old waste places: thou shalt raise up the foundations of many

---

5. Revelation 5:9 " And they sung a new song, saying, Thou art worthy to take the book, and to open the seals thereof: for thou wast slain, and hast redeemed us to God by thy blood out of every kindred, and tongue, and people, and nation;"

generations; and thou shalt be called, The repairer of the breach, The restorer of paths to dwell in. [6]

But he then continues and tells them how they are to do that in the next verses:

If thou turn away thy foot from the sabbath, from doing thy pleasure on my holy day; and call the sabbath a delight, the holy of the LORD, honourable; and shalt honour him, not doing thine own ways, nor finding thine own pleasure, nor speaking thine own words: Then shalt thou delight thyself in the LORD; and I will cause thee to ride upon the high places of the earth, and feed thee with the heritage of Jacob thy father: for the mouth of the LORD hath spoken it. [7]

The way that we are to restore the foundation and build up the walls is to restore the honoring of the Sabbath. To honor the Sabbath is not just the practice of keeping it, but delighting in it. If we want to restore the breaches, what we need to do is recognize the worthlessness of our own pleasures. If we take God's holy day and make it another day off to pursue our pleasures, we are continuing to destroy the foundation. To raise up the foundations, we must stop doing what is right in our own eyes and instead call the Sabbath a delight.

Consider what God is saying here. He is saying that it is important for us to call it a delight. When the foundations of the faith are cracking, we are to start by doing what God has commanded us to do, rather than doing our pleasures, and to add to that, calling it a delight. This does not even mean

6. Isaiah 58:12,
7. Isaiah 58:13-14,

that we have to actually delight in it at first, but we are to say that it is a delight and the holy of the Lord and honorable. Especially as we start to keep the Sabbath holy, it is important to use those words, that it is a delight, then God will bless that desire and make it a delight. The words are important, especially when a father speaks to his household. Each of the children is going to want to go their own way, but the father needs to proclaim to them that it is a holy day and that they need to delight in it. Then they need to turn aside from their normal patterns, such as doing whatever they want and trying to find pleasure where they think it will be, rather than where God says that it is. They need to turn to choosing to speak about things of God rather than their own pursuits; then God will give them delight in Him. Not only that, but God will let them ride on the high places of the earth. They will even have earthly success and joys. They will be fed with the heritage of Jacob. They will receive the land and all manner of blessings. Then they get what they desired at the beginning of verse 13 – to desire to keep the Sabbath, if they pursue God. In other words:

> But seek ye first the kingdom of God, and his righteousness; and all these things shall be added unto you.[8]

God knows what we need, but yet we are to get it by pursuing the kingdom of God which is where all the true good things are.

True Delight

We are also told in these verses that if we want to find delight in the Sabbath, we need to not follow our own ways.

---

8. Matthew 6:33.

This means to not continue to live the same lifestyle on the Sabbath as on every other day of the week. The Sabbath day is to be dramatically different from other days if we are to delight in it. If we treat it like any other day, all of our days will be miserable. We are also to not find our own pleasure. God has told us the pleasure that is to be enjoyed on that day. The pleasure of being with our husband. That pleasure should be in studying God's word and meditating upon it, praying to God, fellowshipping with other brothers and sisters in Christ, showing the pure religion by helping widows and orphans, worshiping in song, and any other pursuit that moves the focus of the day from ourselves and onto God. Not only are we to not actually do our own pleasures, we are to actively constrain the subjects that we talk about, otherwise while we are not pursuing them in deed, we would be in our thoughts and discussions. The Sabbath was made to talk about things of God, not about the difficulties or pleasures of your life, unless it is focused on what God is doing and not what man is attempting to do.

True Recreation

When we hear from the Westminster Confession of Faith that we are to "not only observe an holy rest all the day from their own works, words, and thoughts about their worldly employments and recreations,"[9] it is easy for us to say that is very restrictive. It is important for us to learn from the Sabbath that God's ways are truly pleasant. When we make a pattern of fulfilling joy through the flesh in sport, we will miss the greater joy of spending time with our Creator.

---

9. *Westminster Confession of Faith*, Chapter 20, Paragraph 8.

When we consider as a society how much time we spend in recreation, but yet remain dissatisfied as a people, we need to understand that our recreation is not true recreation. The idea of recreation is to restore ourselves to what we should be. In other words, to be made new again. The sports and entertainment that we pursue as a society has not made us new, but quite the contrary. It has led us down a path where we accept what is evil if it is done by certain classes of individuals. We need to understand that true recreation comes from spending time with God. That is how our strength will be restored. That is the place of true delight.

When we do the things that God has commanded us to do, God will fill us with pleasure in His presence and we will worship Him. O may God give us delight in His holy day!

CHAPTER 11

The Practice

When we consider how the Sabbath is to be a blessing and a delight, that can sound impossible. In many homes, the most stressful time of the week is Sunday morning. The schedule is different than normal. You do not want to be disruptive by entering the church service late. You know that your heart should be at peace before you enter the church, but still the children are arguing and your response to it is not as holy as it should be. Everyone walks into church with a frown on their face. How can this day be a delight? In previous generations when keeping the Sabbath was habitual, people knew how to deal with these things because they were the practices that they had seen while growing up. Now as we have rejected the keeping of the Sabbath and shortened the length of time that we do keep it, the understanding of how to keep our affections on God for a day are no longer available. Because of this need, in this chapter we are going to make some practical suggestions. These suggestions are not a list of things to do as much as they are techniques on how we and people we know have managed some of these issues in their households.

Weekly Preparation

One of the things that can make it difficult to focus on God on the Sabbath is children who are not able to spend that much time focusing on anything, especially anything related to God. We need to consider the Sabbath the culmination of the week, just as it was in the creation week. We are to be doing the work God has given us, but we also have a responsibility to worship God continually. If we and our children are going to be restful on the Sabbath, we need to have a pattern in our daily lives of resting in God. The practice of gathering together as a family for the reading of the Word, praying, teaching, and singing in the home should make the Sunday service more delightful to the participants, because Sunday is a culmination of the worship that has happened in the home only with more brothers and sisters in Christ.

This daily practice should also create opportunities where discipline issues can be resolved, both self-discipline and child discipline, before the Sunday worship service. If you are not able to worship in your home during the week, you need to understand why you can not and fix the problem. If it is distractions, determine how to eliminate those distractions. If it is lack of understanding, do the studying necessary to understand. If it is an inability to sit still, work to increase your patience. Even though we were created to worship God, with our fallen nature we need to work to overcome the infirmities of our flesh. By working to truly worship God in our homes, we are able to enjoy the Sabbath as we should and delight in the gathering of God's people, because it is an extension of our normal practice.

In regards to children, through the worship in the home

during the week, they will develop the ability to attend to the things of God. If a child is not being exposed to worship, when they gather on Sunday they are going to have difficulty in paying attention to something that is foreign to them. Also, during that time of worship during the week, they will need to learn how to sit still and pay attention. During the training period for a child who is not used to this practice, this will involve chastisement, but that will develop patience in them for what will likely be a longer period on the Sabbath.

Another thing that robs the delight of the Sabbath is practices during the week that strengthen the lust of the flesh, the lust of the eyes and the pride of life.[1] If we are constantly engaging our flesh and our sin nature during the week, we are not going to enjoy Sunday when we should make a specific effort to remove even the things of the world that cause those temptations. If we are constantly listening to rock music, the hymns of the faith are going to be boring. Where we spend our time leads to our tastes. If we are always tasting things that do not have a Godward focus, then when we experience the good things of God, they are not going to be worldly enough for our tastes. Of course, God has commanded that we not be delighting in the things of this world, but in God. So when our pleasure all week is coming from the world, we are robbing ourselves of the joys that God has for us on the Sabbath and exchanging them for lesser joys that are but for a moment.

In addition to keeping a Godward focus in the home, children need to be prepared to be engaged on Sunday

---

1.   1 John 2:16 "For all that is in the world, the lust of the flesh, and the lust of the eyes, and the pride of life, is not of the Father, but is of the world."

morning. One of the methods to keep them engaged is for them to be able to understand the sermon and what is happening in the church service. At a church where the preaching goes sequentially through a book of the Bible or the topics of the messages are announced ahead of time, this can be done by reviewing the passages beforehand with your children. If the songs that will be sung can also be known ahead of time, going over them with your children and talking about the meaning of them can make the worship service more engaging to them. By guiding them to understand and be engaged in worship during the week, the Sabbath should stop being about a man that is talking about incomprehensible things and become an anticipated time of learning for them. Expecting your children to take notes and write questions during the sermon can aid in attentiveness. After the sermon, asking them questions, and giving them an opportunity to ask their questions, will allow you to find out their level of comprehension which will give you better insight on how to prepare them for the following week. Also, it gives them an incentive to pay attention, so that they can know the answers.

Preparation Day

The tone for how the Sabbath is kept is usually determined by the activities of the day before. To have an enjoyable rest requires diligence in preparation. Too often, we want to think that we have no choice but to go to the gas station to buy gas simply because we forgot to purchase it the day before. This is not the equivalence of the ox in the ditch. It is a sin. By considering the things that you will need for the Sabbath day, including gasoline, food, and church supplies the day before, you are choosing to be a blessing to those around you. Other things that should be done include gathering the things that your family will need for worship service on Saturday. The scramble to find notebooks, Bibles and coats can turn the Sabbath into anything but restful. Even laying out the clothes for children can reduce the stress Sunday morning. Putting shoes by the door when everyone is inside on Saturday evening can eliminate the last minute scramble Sunday morning when everyone is trying to get out the door. God is a God of order and the more we put things in order on Saturday, the more we can enjoy the time with God on Sunday.

Another thing that is helpful to do the day before the Sabbath is meal preparation. Not that we are forbidden to prepare meals on the Sabbath, but it can make the day more restful if much of the food is already prepared. Some meal preparation and serving can only be done on the day which it is eaten, but there are many types of food that can largely be prepared the day before. By doing those things before the Sabbath, it keeps the focus on worshiping God as much as possible.

These practices can appear to be taking time away from the many things that are being done on a Saturday. But the question to ask is: "How many of those things actually fall into the biblical category of labor?" Too often, we tend to be a people who want to pursue our own pleasures rather than the will of God. If that takes away from our recreation, we need to understand that these preparations are actually part of the work that God has given us to do. It is carrying forward the pattern that God set when He commanded the

Israelites to gather twice as much manna on the sixth day.[2] If we want to delight in Sunday, as we have been commanded, we need to understand that this should and will affect our Saturday.

Sabbath Day Evening

The other things that affect our Sunday is how we celebrate the Sabbath on Saturday evening. If we push the limits on when the Sabbath starts, we will end up getting to bed late with our focus on things other than God. If we start the Sabbath when God has commanded, at sunset on Saturday, then on Sunday morning we begin with having already put aside the stresses of work for hours. It is good to make the routine on Saturday night distinctly different from the rest of the week. It is an evening that should be spent worshiping God. Sometimes we have studied theological books on Saturday evenings as well as doing our typical devotions. One of the important things is to actively declare, whether in prayer, teaching or song, that the Sabbath was given for the good of man and it should be a time of delighting in God. We are told to call the Sabbath a delight[3] and we should literally do that if we desire our families to delight in the Lord. The most important thing is to remember that God has sanctified this time as holy and Saturday evening should be used as a time to worship Him, most typically at a family level.

---

2. Exodus 16:5 "And it shall come to pass, that on the sixth day they shall prepare that which they bring in; and it shall be twice as much as they gather daily."
3. Isaiah 58:13 "If thou turn away thy foot from the sabbath, from doing thy pleasure on my holy day; and call the sabbath a delight, the holy of the LORD, honourable; and shalt honour him, not doing thine own ways, nor finding thine own pleasure, nor speaking thine own words:"

Worship Service

It might appear easy for us to keep the Sabbath during the worship service, because it is during that time that most of the church thinks they are obeying the commandment to keep the Sabbath. But frequently, it can also be a chore to survive rather than a delight to enjoy. If the Sunday worship service is not a time of delight for Christians, we typically see it being because of one of two reasons. Either there is an unruly child that is making worship difficult or the preacher is not sufficiently engaging.

For the unruly child, the parent needs to understand that sitting with a wiggling child on their lap for the worship service distracts from what they are to be about. One response could be to send the child out of the worship service, but then the child is now not fulfilling the obligation that every person has which is to worship the holy God on His holy day. Instead, parents have a responsibility to correct the problem and restore the child to the meeting of the church. God has given parents the rod of correction to drive the foolishness out of the heart of a child.[4] When the child wiggles and does not focus to the best of their ability on the things that are taking place in regards to worship, it is appropriate and necessary to use the rod. The use of the rod should be done quickly, not after much struggling with the child and a level of frustration is reached. It should be used hard enough to change behavior.[5] As a parent, we need to understand the use of the rod is both a mercy to the child and

---

4. Proverbs 22:15 "Foolishness is bound in the heart of a child; but the rod of correction shall drive it far from him."
5. Proverbs 20:20 "The blueness of a wound cleanseth away evil: so do stripes the inward parts of the belly."

an act of obedience to God, which by its nature is worship. After the use of the rod, it is important to move the child back into the worship service as quickly as possible after they gain control of themselves. This is because it is their duty to worship God, so the goal needs to be to get them back into obedience as quickly as possible. Disciplining in this manner is not an immediate fix. But with consistency, the child can be trained so that both the parent and the child are blessed by being able to worship God with the rest of the body of Christ.

The other problem is listening to what is perceived as poor preaching, which can lead the focus from the worship of God to critiquing the pastor. Obviously, there is a point where the teaching is another gospel and should not be heard, but typically the situation is that the preacher is not as gifted as another that you might have heard. In the age of the internet, it is easy to listen to some men that have been a tremendous blessing to the church with their gift of preaching and to measure your local pastor by that standard. But the reason that your local pastor should be more significant in your life is not because of any preaching gifts that he might have, but because God has given him a responsibility to give an accounting for your soul.[6] Because this authority and responsibility is from God, his preaching is blessed by God. It is not the power of the preacher that changes those who hear, but the power of the Holy Spirit. Therefore, whenever you come to hear the Word preached, you should come with a desire and expectation to hear from the living God, not a

6. Hebrews 13:17 "Obey them that have the rule over you, and submit yourselves: for they watch for your souls, as they that must give account, that they may do it with joy, and not with grief: for that is unprofitable for you."

man that is preaching. We are to be like the Bereans and verify the things that are being said against scripture,[7] so if you want the Sabbath to be a delight, you need to move your focus from what the preacher is saying to what God is telling you through his sermon. Instead of critiquing the pastor, be thankful that God still speaks through fallen men, even through bad sermons. Then you can understand the presence of God and therefore worship.

Sunday Afternoon

Once the worship service is over, another opportunity can be easily lost to celebrate the Sabbath. Unless the father and mother in a household are diligent to prevent it, the children can easily go on to things where God is ignored. Depending on the age and maturity of the children, it might even be necessary to provide for some release of energy, in order to facilitate continuing to celebrate the Sabbath. Some running around to release energy after being forced to sit still for a long period of time might be necessary. One concept that is to be borne in mind is that the Sabbath was made to be a blessing to man. We need to be certain that while our expectations should be high for our children, those expectations should not end up making the day a day of torture for them rather than joy. If the time is left unplanned where the children are expected to sit still and meditate, it will be difficult for them and not joyous. On the other hand, we must still remember that the Sabbath is not a day for recreation,

---

7. Acts 17:10-11 "And the brethren immediately sent away Paul and Silas by night unto Berea: who coming thither went into the synagogue of the Jews. These were more noble than those in Thessalonica, in that they received the word with all readiness of mind, and searched the scriptures daily, whether those things were so."

rather to worship and delight in God, even for our unsaved children. So while they may need to expend energy, that time must still be focused on God and not on recreation and things of this world.

There are good activities that can be planned for Sunday afternoon that honor the Sabbath and keep the children engaged in it. One is fellowshipping with other families. God has called us many times in the New Testament to show hospitality to one another.[8] There is no better time to show hospitality than Sunday afternoon. By the adults diligently working to remember the Sabbath day, both families can be encouraged and edified to love and good works. Also, a time with the family in prayer, especially prayers of thanksgiving, is very appropriate. Taking a walk and considering the work of God's hand in the world that He has created could be a good way to honor the Sabbath. Having the family do a Bible study, having a time of catechizing the children or discussing the morning's sermon is very appropriate. The important thing to remember on Sunday afternoon is that it needs to be orderly for small children or keeping the Sabbath will quickly be lost.

If You are Commanded Otherwise

One situation in which it is difficult to keep the Sabbath is when those who are in authority over you command you to work. These situations are difficult to handle because you have the responsibility to submit and show honor to those who are over you, but yet you also have an obligation to obey God rather than man. We should first understand who has

---

8.   Romans 12:13 "Distributing to the necessity of saints; given to hospitality."

the primary responsibility for ensuring that the Sabbath is kept:

> *But the seventh day is the sabbath of the LORD thy God: in it thou shalt not do any work, thou, nor thy son, nor thy daughter, nor thy manservant, nor thy maidservant, nor thine ox, nor thine ass, nor any of thy cattle, nor thy stranger that is within thy gates; that thy manservant and thy maidservant may rest as well as thou.*[9]

It is the head of household's responsibility to ensure that no one under his jurisdiction works, except works of necessity. If we have been given work to do that we believe is wrong to do on the Lord's Day, it is not reasonable for us to put our judgment over that of the authority who God has put over us. If it is blatant disregard of the law of God, we should make an appeal to the authority. But in the end, the words that command obedience for a child to his parent[10] or a wife to her husband[11] are very strong, so there would be few cases where the one in submission should refuse to obey.

In other circumstances such as in employment, the situation frequently is simpler. Trust in God for your provision. Seek a job that does not require employment on God's holy day. As a young man considers what work he should do to further the kingdom of God, a fundamental consideration should be whether it will require working on the Sabbath. If it is not a field such as medicine which does works of mercy,

---

9. Deuteronomy 5:14.
10. Colossians 3:20 "Children, obey your parents in all things: for this is well pleasing unto the Lord."
11. Ephesians 5:22 "Wives, submit yourselves unto your own husbands, as unto the Lord."

choose a different profession to pursue. If you are in a job and are being forced to work on the Sabbath, our encouragement would be to seek other employment. Be willing to take a cut in pay. Be willing to risk being out of work by requesting the day off. It would be hard to look at the scriptures and say that it is always sin for someone to submit to an unrighteous authority. But you need to remember that you will stand before God and answer the question, "What did you love so much that you would not give it up for me?" We are commanded to lay down our life for Christ,[12] so are you willing to give up that job for Him? Are you willing to make less money for Him? The blessing to you and your family will be a far more valuable treasure as you spend the day with God and His people as He has commanded.

Worth the Cost

It can seem daunting to change a lifestyle to keep the Sabbath, but the benefits are also enormous. The American Christian church typically is weak on both doctrine and practice. By setting aside the time that God commands us, there is a tremendous increase in the amount of time that we spend remembering that the world was created by God for God's glory and not for ours. As we spend time contemplating the Creator of the universe and walking in His ways, God will bring us to the greatest joys in this world, such as delighting in the Sabbath:

Then shalt thou delight thyself in the LORD; and I will cause thee to ride upon the high places of the earth,

---

12. Luke 9:23 "And he said to them all, If any man will come after me, let him deny himself, and take up his cross daily, and follow me."

and feed thee with the heritage of Jacob thy father: for the mouth of the LORD hath spoken it.[13]

---

13. Isaiah 58:14

CHAPTER 12

The Exhortation

The purpose of writing this book is not to give interesting information about the Sabbath. The purpose of writing this book is to exhort people who call themselves by the name of Christ to change their ways. The church in America widely believes that things are getting worse and that is to be expected until Christ returns. However, that was not the predominant view of the church throughout history.

The Church's Victory

If we knew of a husband who had the power to aid his wife, to encourage his wife and to rescue his wife from any kind of problem that may arise, and he sat back and watched the situation get worse and worse, doing nothing to help her, we would say that husband would be abusing his wife. That he was a horrible husband. Yet, we accuse Jesus Christ of doing the same thing and consider ourselves righteous. We have promises from scripture that He is not sitting back and letting His church decay, instead we have a promise of His love and the effect of it:

> *Husbands, love your wives, even as Christ also loved the church, and gave himself for it; That he might*

sanctify and cleanse it with the washing of water by the word, That he might present it to himself a glorious church, not having spot, or wrinkle, or any such thing; but that it should be holy and without blemish.[1]

When we say that we should expect the church to be defiled, it is like expecting a man to drag his wife through the mud on the way to the altar. May it never be! Christ does allow the church to go through periods of tribulation to purify her and to strengthen her doctrine, so that in the end the church will be pure, spotless and victorious. We need to understand what the other choice is. The other choice is that we love our sin more than we love God. We love the world and the things of the world[2] more than we love God. The visible church today professes with her tongue that she loves God, but testifies with her actions that her heart is far from Him. When we look at the mainstream church, it is not a group of people that are being sanctified by God for His glory. Instead, we see a love for the world and the things of this world in the church. That is why repentance for our treatment of the Sabbath is so important.

Servants of God Keep the Sabbath

In Isaiah, we are told what it means to join ourselves to the Lord:

Also the sons of the stranger, that join themselves to the LORD, to serve him, and to love the name of the LORD,

---

1. Ephesians 5:25-27.
2. 1 John 2:15 "Love not the world, neither the things that are in the world. If any man love the world, the love of the Father is not in him."

to be his servants, every one that keepeth the sabbath
from polluting it, and taketh hold of my covenant;[3]

When we are saved by believing in the Lord Jesus Christ, we know that we are servants of God.[4] Those who are strangers, meaning not Israelites, who join themselves to the Lord and love the name of the Lord and take hold of God's covenant, keep from polluting the Sabbath. If you believe that you have done and are doing those things, but do not keep the Sabbath, now is the day to repent and proclaim the glories of God. When we think of loving His name, we must understand that has to do with loving His reputation, loving being part of His household, desiring to be called a Christian, but it also means to delight in the rules of the house that God has declared to us in the Bible. God has said that to love Him is to keep His commandments.[5] When we call any of His commandments grievous, such as the Sabbath, we are saying that not only do we not love the name of the Lord, but that we actually hate it. We need to turn and once again say "What a great and marvelous God we have that even though He has every right to call us to work as His servants every minute of every day, He instead calls us to a day of rest. He calls us to spend time with Him and He delights in that time as only a father can delight in spending time with His children, and as a child can delight in spending time with his father." Why

---

3. Isaiah 56:6.

4. Romans 12:1 " I beseech you therefore, brethren, by the mercies of God, that ye present your bodies a living sacrifice, holy, acceptable unto God, which is your reasonable service."

5. 1 John 5:3 "For this is the love of God, that we keep his commandments: and his commandments are not grievous."

would we want to rob God of that? Why would we want to rob ourselves of that?

Confessions of Faith

Many churches today have the Westminster Confession of Faith or the Second London Baptist Confession of Faith as their confessions. Both of these confessions have a chapter which describes the orthodox biblical doctrine of the Sabbath.[6] But many of those that hold to biblical teaching on the Sabbath with their mouths still violate the Sabbath without thinking about their actions. We need to be a people that understand the importance of our witness in respect to keeping the Sabbath. We are in a nation where the citizens are becoming slaves to the state, because we have not trusted God and have not been maintaining a testimony that we are God's people. The state is encroaching on every area of our society, and the reason is partly because we have not been proclaiming that we are being sanctified by God, and He alone has the right to encroach on every area of our lives. To those outside the church, the Sabbath is one of the most obvious witnesses that we are a people who have been set apart. If we expect our nation to change, our churches need to repent and start by both practicing and holding their members accountable to a biblical view of the Sabbath.

Calling to Repentance

The churches need to change their ways not because of some legalistic desire, but because God says this is what His people do. When those people who profess Christ refuse to

---

6. *The Westminster Confession of Faith*, chapter 21 and *The Second London Baptist Confession of Faith of 1689*, chapter 22.

obey the Sabbath, every loving brother has the responsibility to call them to repentance so he does not become complicit in their sin, but also to warn them because they may have deceived themselves that they are actually Christians. When the church fails to discipline in such matters, we are saying that our brother's feelings are more important to us than if our brother goes to hell. That is not the form of love that we are called to in God's Word. We are called to a love that should have concern about our brother. We need to be a people who warn our brother when he is on a path of destruction. Despising the Sabbath is part of the path to destruction.

God's Kindness in Giving us the Sabbath

However, the path of righteousness is always the more pleasant path. Because most of our church practices are focused on an hour or two Sunday morning, we need to re-establish practices where the people of God delight in their time together and spend time with one another like brothers and sisters. The typical practices in today's church might give some time for interaction with one another during the Sunday school hour, but how much more can we encourage one another to love and good works, if we obey God's commandment to set aside twenty-four hours just to delight in God and in the church? God has truly been kind to us in how He has commanded us to set aside a day once a week and move our focus from the things that are related to surviving and enjoying the things of this world, and focus on Him and His people. May we learn to find delight where God has called us to delight.

Psalm 92

A Psalm or Song for the sabbath day.

It is a good thing to give thanks unto the LORD,

and to sing praises unto thy name, O most High:

To shew forth thy lovingkindness in the morning,

and thy faithfulness every night,

Upon an instrument of ten strings,

and upon the psaltery;

upon the harp with a solemn sound.

For thou, LORD, hast made me glad through thy work:

I will triumph in the works of thy hands.

O LORD, how great are thy works!

and thy thoughts are very deep.

A brutish man knoweth not;

neither doth a fool understand this.

When the wicked spring as the grass,

and when all the workers of iniquity do flourish;

it is that they shall be destroyed for ever:

But thou, LORD, art most high for evermore.

For, lo, thine enemies, O LORD,

for, lo, thine enemies shall perish;

all the workers of iniquity shall be scattered.

But my horn shalt thou exalt like the horn of an unicorn:

I shall be anointed with fresh oil.

Mine eye also shall see my desire on mine enemies,

and mine ears shall hear my desire of the wicked

that rise up against me.

The righteous shall flourish like the palm tree:
he shall grow like a cedar in Lebanon.
Those that be planted in the house of the LORD
shall flourish in the courts of our God.
They shall still bring forth fruit in old age;
they shall be fat and flourishing;
To shew that the LORD is upright: he is my rock, and there
is no unrighteousness in him.

The Perpetuity and Change of the Sabbath

Jonathan Edwards (1703-1758)

"Now concerning the collection for the saints, as I have given order to the churches of Galatia, even so do ye. Upon the first day of the week, let every one of you lay by him in store, as God hath prospered him, that there be no gatherings when I come."

1 Corinthians 16:1-2

Subject

That it is the mind and will of God that the first day of the week should be the day that should be especially set apart for religious exercises and duties among Christians.

We find in the New Testament often mentioned a certain collection, which was made by the Grecian churches, for the brethren in Judea, who were reduced to pinching want by a dearth which then prevailed, and was the heavier upon them by reason of their circumstances, they having been from the beginning oppressed and persecuted by the unbelieving Jews. This collection or contribution is twice mentioned in the Acts, 11:28-30 and 24:17. It is also noticed in several of the epistles: as Rom. 15:26 and Gal. 2:10. But it is most largely insisted on, in these two epistles to the Corinthians: in this first epistle, 16, and in the second epistle, 8 and 9. The apostle begins the directions, which in this place he delivers concerning this matter, with the words of the text — wherein we may observe,

I. What is the thing to be done concerning which the apostle gives them direction — the exercise and manifestation of their charity towards their brethren — by communicating to them for the supply of their wants, which was by Christ and his apostles often insisted on, as one main duty of the Christian religion and is expressly declared to be so by the apostle James, chap. 1:27, "Pure religion and undefiled before God and the Father is this, to visit the fatherless and widows in their affliction."

II. We may observe the time on which the apostle directs that this should be done, *viz.* "on the first day of the week." By the inspiration of the Holy Ghost he insists upon it, that it be done on such a particular day of the week, as if no other day would do so well as that, or were so proper and fit a time for such a work. — Thus, although the inspired apostle was not for making that distinction of days in gospel times, which the Jews made, as appears by Gal. 4:10, "Ye observe days, and months," etc., yet here he gives the preference to one day of the week, before any other, for the performance of a certain great duty of Christianity.

III. It may be observed that the apostle had given to other churches, that were concerned in the same duty, to do it on the first day of the week: "As I have given orders to the churches of Galatia, even so do ye." Whence we may learn, that it was nothing peculiar in the circumstances of the Christians at Corinth, which was the reason why the Holy ghost insisted that they should perform this duty *on this day* of the week. The apostle had given the like orders to the churches of Galatia.

Now Galatia was far distant from Corinth: the sea parted them, and there were several other countries between them. Therefore it cannot be thought that the Holy Ghost directs them to this time upon any *secular* account, having respect to some particular circumstances of the people in that city, but upon a *religious* account. In giving the preference to this day for such work, before any other day, he has respect to something which reached all Christians throughout the wide world.

And by other passages of the New Testament, we learn that the case was the same as to other exercises of religion, and that the first day of the week was preferred before any other day, in churches immediately under the care of the apostles, for an attendance on the exercises of religion in general. Acts 20:7, "Upon the first day of the week, when the disciples came together to break bread, Paul preached unto them." It seems by these things to have been among the primitive Christians in the apostles' days, with respect to the first day of the week, as it was among the Jews, with respect to the seventh.

We are taught by Christ, that the doing of alms and showing of mercy are proper works for the Sabbath-day. When the Pharisees found fault with Christ for suffering his disciples to pluck the ears of corn, and eat on the Sabbath, Christ corrects them with that saying, "I will have mercy and not sacrifice;" Mat. 12:7. And Christ teaches that works of mercy are proper to be done on the Sabbath, Luke 13:15, 16, and 14:5. — These works used to be done on sacred festivals and days of rejoicing under the Old Testament, as in Nehemiah's and Esther's time, Neh. 8:10 and Est. 9:19, 22. — And Josephus and Philo, two very noted Jews, who wrote not long after Christ's time, give an account that it was the manner among the Jews on the Sabbath, to make collections for sacred and pious uses.

DOCTRINE

It is the mind and will of God that the first day of the week should be especially set apart among Christians for religious exercises and duties.

That this is the doctrine which the Holy Ghost intended to teach us, by this and some other passages of the New Testament, I hope will appear plainly by the sequel. This is a doctrine that we have been generally brought up in by the instructions and examples of our ancestors, and it has been the general profession of the Christian world, that this day ought to be religiously observed and distinguished from other days of the week. However, some deny it. Some refuse to take notice of the day, as different from other days. Others own that it is a laudable custom of the Christian church, into which she fell by agreement and by appointment of her ordinary rulers, to set apart this day for public worship. But they deny any other original to such an observation of the day, than prudential human appointment. Others religiously observe the Jewish Sabbath, as of perpetual obligation, and that we want a foundation for determining that that is abrogated, and another day of the week is appointed in the room of the seventh.

All these classes of men say that there is no clear revelation that it is the mind and will of God, that the first day of the week should be observed as a day to be set apart for religious exercises, in the room of the ancient Sabbath, which there ought to be in order to the observation of it by the Christian church as a divine institution. They say that we ought not to go upon the tradition of past ages, or upon uncertain and far-fetched inferences from some passages of the history of the New Testament, or upon some obscure and uncertain hints in the apostolic writings. But that we ought to expect a plain institution, which they say we may conclude God would have given us, if he had designed that the whole Christian church, in all ages, should observe another day of the week for a holy Sabbath, than that which was appointed of old by plain and positive institution.

So far it is undoubtedly true that if this be the mind and will of God, he has not left the matter to human tradition, but has so revealed his mind about it, in his Word, that there is to be found good and substantial evidence that it is his mind. Doubtless, the revelation is plain enough for them that have ears to hear: that is for them that will justly exercise their understandings about what God says to them. No Christian, therefore, should rest till he has satisfactorily discovered the mind of God in this matter. If the Christian Sabbath be of divine institution, it is doubtless of great importance to religion that it be well kept, and therefore, that every Christian be well acquainted with the institution.

If men take it only upon trust, and keep the first day of the week because their parents taught them so, or because they see others do it, they will never be likely to keep it so conscientiously and strictly, as if they had been convinced by seeing for themselves that there are good grounds in the Word of God for their practice. Unless they do see thus for themselves, whenever they are negligent in sanctifying the Sabbath or are guilty of profaning it, their consciences will not have that advantage to smite them for it, as otherwise they would. — And those who have a sincere desire to obey God in all things, will keep the Sabbath more carefully and more cheerfully, if they have seen and been convinced that therein they do what is according to the will and command of God, and what is acceptable to him. [They] will also have a great deal more comfort in the reflection upon their having carefully and painfully kept the Sabbath.

Therefore, I design now, by the help of God, to show that it is sufficiently revealed in the Scriptures, to be the mind and will of God, that the first day of the week should be distinguished in the Christian church from other days of the week, as a Sabbath, to be devoted to religious exercises.

In order to this, I shall here premise that the mind and will of God, concerning any duty to be performed by us, may be sufficiently revealed in his Word, without a particular precept in so many express terms, enjoying it. The human understanding is the ear to which the Word of God is spoken; and if it be so spoken, that *that* ear may plainly hear it, it is enough. God is sovereign as to the manner of speaking his mind, whether he will speak it in express terms, or whether he will speak it by saying several other things which imply it, and from which we may, by comparing them together, plainly perceive it. If the mind of God be but revealed, if there be but sufficient means for the communication of his mind to our minds, that is sufficient: whether we hear so many express words with our ears, or see them in writing with our eyes, or whether we see the thing that he would signify to us, by the eye of reason and understanding.

Who can positively say that if it had been the mind of God, that we should keep the first day of the week, he would have commanded it in express terms, as he did the observation of the seventh day of old? Indeed, if God had so made our faculties, that we were not capable of receiving a revelation of his mind in any other way, then there would have been some reason to say so. But God has given us such understandings, that we are capable of receiving a revelation, when made in another manner. And if God deals with us agreeably to our natures, and in a way suitable to our capacities, it is enough. If God discovers his mind in any way whatsoever, provided it be according to our faculties, we are obliged to obedience, and God may expect our notice and observance of his revelation, in the same manner as if he had revealed it in express terms.

I shall speak upon this subject under these two general propositions.

I. It is sufficiently clear, that it is the mind of God, that one day of the week should be devoted to rest, and to religious exercises, throughout all ages and nations.

II. It is sufficiently clear, that under the gospel-dispensation, this day is the first day of the week.

I. Prop. It is sufficiently clear that it is the mind of God, that one day of the week should be devoted to rest and to religious exercises, throughout all ages and nations: not only among the ancient Israelites, till Christ came, but even in these gospel times and among all nations professing Christianity.

First, from the consideration of the nature and state of mankind in this world, it is most consonant to human reason that certain fixed parts of time should be set apart, to be spent by the church wholly in religious exercises, and in the duties of divine worship. It is a duty incumbent on all mankind, in all ages alike, to worship and serve God. His service should be our great business. It becomes us to worship him with the greatest devotion and engagedness of mind, and therefore to put ourselves, at proper times, in such circumstances as will most contribute to render our minds entirely devoted to this work, without being diverted or interrupted by other things.

The state of mankind in this world is such that we are called to concern ourselves in secular business and affairs, which will necessarily, in a considerable degree, take up the thoughts and engage the attention of the mind. However, some particular persons may be in circumstances more free and disengaged. Yet the state of mankind is such that the bulk of them, in all ages and nations, are called ordinarily to exercise their thoughts about secular affairs, and to follow worldly business, which in its own nature, is remote from the solemn duties of religion.

It is therefore most meet and suitable that certain times should be set apart, upon which men should be required to throw by all other concerns: that their minds may be the more freely and entirely engaged in spiritual exercises in the duties of religion and in the immediate worship of God, and that their minds being disengaged from common concerns, their religion may not be mixed with them.

It is also suitable that these times should be fixed and settled, that the church may agree therein and that they should be the same for all, that men may not interrupt one another, but may rather assist one another by mutual example: for example has a great influence in such cases. If there be a time set apart for public rejoicing, and there be a general manifestation of joy, the general example seems to inspire men with a spirit of joy: one kindles another. So, if it be a time of mourning, and there be general appearances and manifestations of sorrow, it naturally affects the mind: it disposes it to depression, it casts a gloom upon it, and does as it were dull and deaden the spirits. So, if a certain time be set apart as holy time, for general devotion and solemn religious exercises, a general example tends to render the spirit serious and solemn.

Second, without doubt, one proportion of time is better and fitter than another for this purpose. One proportion is more suitable to the state of mankind and will have a greater tendency to answer the ends of such times, than another. The times may be too far asunder. I think human reason is sufficient to discover that it would be too seldom for the purposes of such solemn times, that they should be but once a year. So, I conclude, nobody will deny but that such times may be too near together to agree with the state and necessary affairs of mankind.

Therefore, there can be no difficulty in allowing that some certain proportion of time, whether we can exactly discover it or not, is really fittest and best — considering the end for which such times are kept, and the condition, circumstances, and necessary affairs of men; and considering what the state of man is, taking one age and nation with another — more convenient and suitable than any other, which God may know and exactly determine, though we, by reason of the scantiness of our understandings, cannot.

As a certain frequency of the returns of these times may be more suitable than any other, so one length or continuance of the times themselves may be fitter than another, to answer the purposes of such times. If such times, when they come, were to last but an hour, it would not well answer the end. For then worldly things would crowd too nearly upon sacred exercises, and there would not be that opportunity to get the mind so thoroughly free and disengaged from other things, as there would be if the times were longer. Being so short, sacred and profane things would be as it were mixed together. Therefore, a certain distance between these times, and a certain continuance of them when they come, is more proper than others, which God knows and is able to determine, though perhaps we cannot.

Third, it is unreasonable to suppose any other, than that God's working six days and resting the seventh, and blessing and hallowing it, was to be of general use in determining this matter. It was written that the practice of mankind in general might some way or other be regulated by it. What could be the meaning of God's resting the seventh day and hallowing and blessing it, which he did before the giving of the fourth commandment, unless he hallowed and blessed it with respect to mankind? For he did not bless and sanctify it with respect to himself, or that he within himself might observe it: as that is most absurd. And it is unreasonable to suppose that he hallowed it only with respect to the Jews, a particular nation, which rose up above two thousand years after.

So much therefore must be intended by it, that it was his mind, that mankind should, after his example, work six days and then rest and hallow or sanctify the next following: that they should sanctify every seventh day, or that the space between rest and rest, one hallowed time and another, among his creatures here upon earth, should be six days. — So that it hence appears to be the mind and will of God that not only the Jews, but man in all nations and ages, should sanctify one day in seven: which is the thing we are endeavoring to prove.

Fourth, the mind of God in this matter is clearly revealed in the fourth commandment. The will of God is there revealed, not only that the Israelitish nation, but that all nations, should keep every seventh day holy, or which is the same thing, one day after every six. This command, as well as the rest, is doubtless everlasting and of perpetual obligation, at least as to the substance of it, as is intimated by its being engraven on the tables of stone. Nor is it to be thought that Christ ever abolished any command of the ten, but that there is the complete number ten yet, and will be to the end of the world.

Some say, that the fourth command is perpetual, but not in its literal sense: not as designing any particular proportion of time to be set apart and devoted to literal rest and religious exercises. They say that it stands in force only in a mystical sense, *viz.* as that weekly rest of the Jews typified spiritual rest in the Christian church, and that we under the gospel are not to make any distinction of one day from another, but are to keep all time holy, doing everything in a spiritual manner.

But this is an absurd way of interpreting the command, as it refers to Christians. For if the command be so far abolished, it is entirely abolished. For it is the very design of the command, to fix the time of worship. The first command fixes the object, the second the means, the third the manner, the fourth the time. And if it stands in force now only as signifying a spiritual, Christian rest, and holy behavior at all times, it does not remain as one of the ten commands, but as a summary of all the commands.

The main objection against the perpetuity of this command is that the duty required is not moral. Those laws whose obligations arises from the nature of things and from the general state and nature of mankind, as well as from God's positive revealed will, are called moral laws. Others, whose obligation depends merely upon God's positive and arbitrary institution, are not moral: such as the ceremonial laws, and the precepts of the gospel about the two sacraments. Now, the objectors say, they will allow all that is moral in the decalogue to be of perpetual obligation. But this command, they say, is not moral.

But this objection is weak and insufficient for the purpose for which it is brought, or to prove that the fourth command, as to the substance of it, is not of perpetual obligation. For,

1. If it should be allowed that there is no morality belonging to the command, and that the duty required is founded merely on arbitrary institution, it cannot therefore be certainly concluded that the command is not perpetual. We know that there may be commands in force under the gospel and to the end of the world, which are not moral. Such are the institutions of the two sacraments. And why may there not be positive commands in force in all ages of the church? If positive, arbitrary institutions are in force in gospel-times, what is there which concludes that no positive precept give before the times of the gospel can yet continue in force? But,

2. As we have observed already, the thing in general that there should be certain fixed parts of time set apart to be devoted to religious exercises, is founded in the fitness of the thing, arising from the nature of things, and the nature and universal state of mankind. Therefore, there is as much reason that there should be a command of perpetual and

universal obligation about this, as about any other duty whatsoever. For if the thing in general, that there be a time fixed, be founded in the nature of things, there is consequent upon it a necessity, that the time be limited by a command. For there must be a proportion of time fixed, or else the general moral duty cannot be observed.

3. The particular determination of the proportion of time in the fourth commandment, is also founded in the nature of things, only our understandings are not sufficient absolutely to determine it of themselves. We have observed already that without doubt one proportion of time is in itself fitter than another, and a certain continuance of time fitter than any other, considering the universal state and nature of mankind, which God may see, though our understandings are not perfect enough absolutely to determine it. So that the difference between this command and others, does not lie in this (that other commands are founded in the fitness of the things themselves, arising from the universal state and nature of mankind, and this not), but only that the fitness of other commands is more obvious to the understandings of men, and they might have seen it of themselves. But this could not be precisely discovered and positively determined without the assistance of revelation.

So that the command of God, that every seventh day should be devoted to religious exercises, is founded in the universal state and nature of mankind, as well as other commands. Only man's reason is not sufficient, without divine direction, so exactly to determine it. Though perhaps man's reason is sufficient to determine that it ought not to be much seldomer, nor much oftener, than once in seven days.

Fifth, God appears in his Word laying abundantly more weight on this precept concerning the Sabbath, than on any precept of the ceremonial law. It is in the decalogue, one of the ten commands, which were delivered by God with an audible voice. It was written with his own finger on the tables of stone in the mount, and was appointed afterwards to be written on the tables which Moses made. The keeping of the weekly Sabbath is spoken of by the prophets, as that wherein consists a great part of holiness of life, and is inserted among moral duties, Isa. 58:13, 14, "If thou turn away thy foot from the sabbath, from doing thy pleasure on my holy day; and call the sabbath a delight, the holy of the Lord, honourable; and shalt honour him, not doing thine own words: then shalt thou delight thyself in the Lord; and I will cause thee to ride upon the high places of the earth, and feed thee with the heritage of Jacob thy father: for the mouth of the Lord hath spoken it."

Sixth, it is foretold that this command should be observed in gospel-times, as in Isa. 56 at the beginning, where the due observance of the

Sabbath is spoken of as a great part of holiness of life, and is placed among moral duties. It is also mentioned as a duty that should be most acceptable to God from his people, even where the prophet is speaking of gospel-times, as in the foregoing chapter, and in the first verse of this chapter. And, in the third and fourth verses, the prophet is speaking of the abolition of the ceremonial law in gospel-times, and particularly of that law, which forbids eunuchs to come into the congregation of the Lord. Yet, here the man is pronounced blessed, who keeps the Sabbath from polluting it, verse 2. And even in the very sentence where the eunuchs are spoken of as being free from the ceremonial law, they are spoken of as being yet under obligation to keep the Sabbath, and actually keeping it, as that which God lays great weight upon: "For thus saith the Lord, unto the eunuchs that keep my sabbaths, and choose the things that please me, and take hold of my covenant; Even unto them will I give in mine house, and within my walls, a place and a name better than of sons and of daughters: I will give them an everlasting name, that shall not be cut off."

Besides, the strangers spoken of in the sixth and seventh verses, are the Gentiles, that should be called in the times of the gospel, as is evident by the last clause in the seventh, and by the eighth verse: "For mine house shall be called an house of prayer for all people. The Lord God, which gathereth the outcasts of Israel, saith, Yet will I gather others to him, besides those that are gathered unto him." Yet it is represented here as their duty to keep the Sabbath: "Also the sons of the stranger, that join themselves to the Lord, to serve him, and to love the name of the Lord, to be his servants, every one that keepeth the sabbath from polluting it, and taketh hold of my covenant; even them will I bring to my holy mountain, and make them joyful in my house of prayer."

Seventh, a further argument for the perpetuity of the Sabbath, we have in Mat. 24:20, "Pray ye that your flight be not in the winter, neither on the sabbath-day." Christ is here speaking of the flight of the apostles and other Christians out of Jerusalem and Judea, just before their final destruction, as is manifest by the whole context, and especially by the 16th verse, "Then let them which be in Judea flee into the mountains." But this final destruction of Jerusalem was after the dissolution of the Jewish constitution, and after the Christian dispensation was fully set up. Yet, it is plainly implied in these words of our Lord, that even then Christians were bound to a strict observation of the Sabbath.

Thus I have shown that it is the will of God that every seventh day be devoted to rest and to religious exercises.

II. Prop. That it is the will of God that under the gospel dispensation, or in the Christian church, this day should be the first day of the week.

In order to the confirmation of this, let the following things be considered.

First, the words of the fourth commandment afford no objections against this being the day that should be the Sabbath, any more than against any other day. That this day, which according to the Jewish reckoning, is the first of the week, should be kept as a Sabbath, is no more opposite to any sentence or word of the fourth command, than that the seventh of the week should be the day. The words of the fourth command do not determine which day of the week we should keep as a Sabbath. They merely determine, that we should rest and keep as a Sabbath every seventh day, or one day after every six. It says, "Six days thou shalt labour, and the seventh thou shalt rest;" which implies no more, than that after six days of labour, we shall upon the next to the sixth, rest and keep it holy. And this we are obliged to do forever. But the words no way determine where those six days shall begin, and so where the rest or Sabbath shall fall. There is no direction in the fourth command how to reckon the time, *i.e.* where to begin and end it. But that is supposed to be determined otherwise.

The Jews did not know, by the fourth command, where to begin their six days, and on which particular day to rest: this was determined by another precept. The fourth command does indeed suppose a particular day appointed; but it does not appoint any. It requires us to rest and keep holy a seventh day, one after every six of labor, which particular day God either had or should appoint. The particular day was determined for that nation in another place, *viz.* in Exo. 16:23-26, "And he said unto them, this is that which the Lord hath said, Tomorrow is the rest of the holy sabbath unto the Lord: bake that which ye will bake, today, and seethe that ye will seethe; and that which remaineth over, lay up for you to be kept until the morning. And Moses said, Eat that today; for today is a sabbath unto the Lord: today ye shall not find it in the field. Six days ye shall gather it; but on the seventh day, which is the sabbath, in it there shall be none." This is the first place where we have any mention made of the Sabbath, from the first Sabbath on which God rested.

It seems that the Israelites, in the time of their bondage in Egypt, had lost the true reckoning of time by the days of the week, reckoning from the first day of the creation. They were slaves and in cruel bondage and had in a great measure forgotten the true religion. For we are told that they served the gods of Egypt. And it is not to be supposed that the Egyptians would suffer their slaves to rest from their work every seventh day. Now, they having remained in bondage for so long a time, had probably lost the weekly reckoning. Therefore, when God had brought them out of

Egypt into the wilderness, he made known to them the Sabbath, on the occasion and in the manner recorded in the text just now quoted. Hence, we read in Nehemiah that when God had led the children of Israel out of Egypt, etc. he made known unto them his holy Sabbath, Neh. 9:14, "And madest known unto them the holy sabbath." To the same effect, we read din Eze. 20:10, 12, "Wherefore I caused them to go forth out of the land of Egypt, and brought them into the wilderness. Moreover also, I gave them my sabbaths."

But they never would have known where the particular day would have fallen by the fourth command. Indeed, the fourth command, as it was spoken to the Jews, did refer to their Jewish Sabbath. But that does not prove that the day was determined and appointed by it. The precept in the fourth command is to be taken generally of such a seventh day as God should appoint, or had appointed. And because such a particular day had been already appointed for the Jewish church, therefore, as it was spoken to them, it did refer to that particular day. But this does not prove, but the same words refer to another appointed seventh day, now in the Christian church. The words of the fourth command may oblige the church, under different dispensations, to observe different appointed seventh days, as well as the fifth command may oblige different persons to honor different fathers and mothers.

The Christian Sabbath, in the sense of the fourth command, is as much the seventh day as the Jewish Sabbath, because it is kept after six days of labor as well as that. It is the seventh reckoning from the beginning of our first working-day, as well as that was the seventh from the beginning of their first working day. All the difference is that the seven days formerly began from the day after God's rest from the creation, and now they begin the day after that. It is no matter by what names the days are called: if our nation had, for instance, called Wednesday the first day of the week, it would have been all one as to this argument.

Therefore, by the institution of the Christian Sabbath, there is no change from the fourth command; but the change is from another law, which determined the beginning and ending of their working days. So that those words of the fourth command, *viz.* "For in six days the Lord made heaven and earth, the sea, and all that in them is, and rested the seventh day; wherefore the Lord blessed the sabbath-day, and hallowed it." These words are not made insignificant to Christians, by the institution of the Christian Sabbath. They still remain in their full force as to that which is principally intended by them. They were designed to give us a reason why we are to work but six days at a time, and then rest on the seventh, because God has set us the example. And taken so, they remain still in as much force as ever they were. This is the reason still, as much as ever it was, why we may work but six days at a time. What is the reason that Christians rest every seventh, and not every eighth, or every ninth, or tenth day? It is because God worked six days and rested the seventh.

It is true, these words did carry something further in their meaning, as they were spoken to the Jews, and to the church before the coming of Christ. It was then also intended by them that the seventh day was to be kept in commemoration of the work of creation. But this is no objection to the supposition that the words, as they relate to us, do not import all that they did, as they related to the Jews. For there are other words which were written upon those tables of stone with the ten commandments, which are known and allowed not to be of the same import, as they relate to us, and as they related to the Jews, *viz.* these words, in the preface to the ten commandments, "I am the Lord thy God, which brought thee out of the land of Egypt, out of the house of bondage." — These words were written on the tables of stone with the rest, and are spoken to us, as well as to the Jews. They are spoken to all to whom the commandments themselves are spoken, for they are spoken as an enforcement of the commandments. But they do not now remain in all the signification which they had, as they respected the Jews. For we never were brought out of Egypt, out of the house of bondage, except in a mystical sense. — The same may be said of those words which are inserted in the commandments themselves, Deu. 5:15, "And remember that thou wast a servant in the land of Egypt, and that the Lord thy God commanded thee out thence, through a mighty hand and by a stretched-out arm: therefore the Lord thy God commanded thee to keep the sabbath-day."

So that all the arguments of those who are against the Christian Sabbath, drawn from the fourth command, which are all their strength, come to nothing.

Second, that the ancient church was commanded to keep a seventh day in commemoration of the work of creation, is an argument for the keeping of a weekly Sabbath in commemoration of the work of redemption, and not any reason against it.

We read in Scripture of two creations, the old and the new, and these words of the fourth command are to be taken as of the same force to those who belong to the new creation, with respect to that new creation as they were to those who belonged to the old creation, with respect to that. We read that "in the beginning God created the heaven and the earth," and the church of old were to commemorate that work. But when God creates a new heaven and a new earth, those that belong to this new heaven and new earth, by a like reason, are to commemorate the creation

149

of their heaven and earth.

The Scriptures teach us to look upon the old creation as destroyed, and as it were annihilated by sin; or, as being reduced to a chaos again, without form and void, as it was at first. Jer. 4:22, 23, "They are wise to do evil, but to do good they have no knowledge. I beheld the earth, and lo, it was without form and void: and the heavens, and they had no light!" *i.e.* were reduced to the same state in which they were at first; the earth was without form and void, and there was no light, but darkness was upon the face of the deep.

The Scriptures further teach us to call the gospel-restoration and redemption, a creation of a new heaven and a new earth; Isa. 65:17, 18, "For behold, I create new heavens, and a new earth; and the former shall not be remembered, nor come into mind. But be you glad and rejoice forever in that which I create: for behold, I create Jerusalem a rejoicing, and her people a joy." And Isa. 51:16, "And I have put my words in thy mouth, and have covered thee in the shadow of mine hand, that I may plant the heavens, and lay the foundations of the earth, and say unto Zion, Thou art my people." And Isa. 66:22, "For as the new heavens and the new earth which I will make," etc. — In these places we are not only told a new creation, or new heavens and a new earth, but we are told what is meant by it, *viz.* The gospel renovation, the making of Jerusalem a rejoicing, and her people a joy, saying unto Zion, "Thou art my people," etc. The prophet, in all these places, is prophesying of the gospel-redemption.

The gospel-state is everywhere spoken of as a renewed state of things, wherein old things are passed away, and all things become new: we are said to be created unto Christ Jesus unto good works. All things are restored and reconciled whether in heaven or in earth, and God has caused light to shine out of darkness, as he did at the beginning. And the dissolution of the Jewish state was often spoken of in the Old Testament as the end of the world. — But we who belong to the gospel-church, belong to the new creation. Therefore there seems to be at least as much reason that we should commemorate the work of this creation, as that the members of the ancient Jewish church should commemorate the work of the old creation.

Third, there is another thing which confirms it (that the fourth command teaches God's resting from the new creation, as well as from the old), which is that the Scriptures expressly speak of the one as parallel with the other: *i.e.* Christ's resting from the work of redemption is expressly spoken of as being parallel with God's resting from the work of creation. Heb. 4:10, "For he that is entered into his rest, he also hath ceased from his own works, as God did from his."

Now Christ rested from his works when he rose from the dead, on the first day of the week. When he rose from the dead, then he finished his work of redemption. His humiliation was then at an end: he then rested and was refreshed. — When it is said, "There remaineth a rest to the people of God;" in the original, it is, a *sabbatism,* or *the keeping of a Sabbath*: and this reason is given for it, "For he that entered into his rest, he also hath ceased from his own works, as God did from his." — These three things at least we are taught by these words:

1. To look upon Christ's rest from his work of redemption, as parallel with God's rest from the work of creation. For they are expressly compared together, as parallel one with the other.

2. They are spoken of as parallel, particularly in this respect, *viz.* the relation which they both have to the keeping of a Sabbath among God's people, or with respect to the influence which these two rests have as to sabbatizing in the church of God. For it is expressly with respect to this that they are compared together. Here is an evident reference to God's blessing and hallowing the day of his rest from the creation to be a Sabbath, and appointing a Sabbath of rest in imitation of him. For the apostle is speaking of this, verse 4, "For he spake in a certain place of the seventh day on this wise, And God did rest the seventh day from all his works." Thus far is evident, whatever the apostle has respect to by this keeping of a Sabbath by the people of God: whether it be a weekly sabbatizing on earth or a sabbatizing in heaven.

3. It is evident in these words that the preference is given to the latter rest, *viz.* the rest of our Savior from his works, with respect to the influence it should have or relation it bears, to the sabbatizing of the people of God, now under the gospel, evidently implied in the expression, "There remaineth therefore a sabbatism to the people of God. For he that entered into his rest," etc. For in this sabbatism appointed in remembrance of God's rest from the work of creation, does not remain, but ceases, and that this new rest, in commemoration of Christ's resting from his works, remains in the room of it.

Fourth, the Holy Ghost has implicitly told us that the Sabbath which was instituted in commemoration of the old creation, should not be kept in gospel-times. Isa. 65:17, 18. There we are told that when God should create new heavens and a new earth, the former should not be remembered, nor come into mind. If this be so, it is not to be supposed that we are to keep a seventh part of time, on purpose to remember it, and call it to mind.

Let us understand this which way we will, it will not be well consistent with the keeping of one day in seven, in the gospel-church, principally for the remembrance and calling to mind of the old creation. If the meaning of the place be only this — that the old creation shall not be remembered nor come into mind in comparison with the *new*, that the *new* will be so much more remarkable and glorious, will so much more nearly concern us, so much more notice will taken of it, and it will be thought so much more worthy to be remembered and commemorated, that the other will not be remembered, nor come into mind — it is impossible that it should be more to our purpose. For then hereby the Holy Ghost teaches us, that the Christian church has much more reason to commemorate the new creation than the old; insomuch, that the old is worthy to be forgotten in comparison with it.

And as the old creation was no more to be remembered, nor come into mind; so, in the following verse, the church is directed forever to commemorate the new creation, "But be you glad, and rejoice for ever in that which I create; for behold, I create Jerusalem a rejoicing, and her people a joy;" *i.e.* Though you forget the old, yet forever to the end of the world, keep a remembrance of the new creation.

Fifth, it is an argument that the Jewish Sabbath was not to be perpetual, that the Jews were commanded to keep it in remembrance of their deliverance out of Egypt. One reason why it was instituted was because God thus delivered them, as we are expressly told, Deu. 5:15, "And remember that thou wast a servant in the land of Egypt, and that the Lord thy God brought thee out thence, through a mighty hand, and by a stretched-out arm: therefore the Lord thy God commanded thee to keep the sabbath-day." Now can any person think that God would have all nations under the gospel, and to the end of the world, keep a day every week, which was instituted in remembrance of the deliverance of the Jews out of Egypt?

Sixth, the Holy Ghost has implicitly told us that instituted memorials of the Jews' deliverance from Egypt should be no longer upheld in gospel-times, Jer. 16:14-15. The Holy Ghost, speaking of gospel-times, says, "Therefore, behold the days come, saith the Lord, that it shall no more be said, The Lord liveth that brought up the children of Israel out of Egypt; but the Lord liveth that brought up the children of Israel from the land of the north, and from all the lands whither he had driven them; and I will bring them again into their own land." *They shall no more say, The Lord liveth that brought, etc. i.e.* at least they shall keep up no more any public memorials of it.

If there be a Sabbath kept up in gospel-times, as we have shown there must be it is more just from these words to suppose that it should be as a memorial of that which is spoken of in the latter verse, *the bringing up of the children of Israel from the land of the north:* that is the redemption of Christ and his bringing home the elect, not only from Judea, but from the north, and from all quarters of the world. — See Isa. 43:16-20.

Seventh, it is no more than just to suppose that God intended to intimate to us that the Sabbath ought by Christians to be kept in commemoration of Christ's redemption, in that the Israelites were commanded to keep it in remembrance of their deliverance out of Egypt, because that deliverance out of Egypt is an evident, known, and allowed type of it. It was ordered of God, on purpose to represent it. Everything about that deliverance was typical of this redemption, and much is made of it, principally for this reason: because it is so remarkable a type of Christ's redemption. And it was but a shadow, the work in itself was nothing in comparison with the work of redemption. What is a petty redemption of one nation from a temporal bondage, to the eternal salvation of the whole church of the elect in all ages and nations, from eternal damnation and the introduction of them, not into a temporal Canaan, but into heaven: into eternal glory and blessedness? Was that shadow so much to be commemorated as that a day once a week was to be kept on the account of it, and shall not we much more commemorate that great and glorious work of which it was designed on purpose to be a shadow.

Besides, the words in the fourth commandment, which speak of the deliverance out of Egypt, can be of no significance unto us, unless they are to be interpreted of the gospel-redemption. But the words of the decalogue are spoken to all nations and ages. Therefore, as the words were spoken to the Jews, they referred to the type or shadow. As they are spoken to us, they are to be interpreted of the antitype and substance. For the Egypt from which we under the gospel are redeemed, is the spiritual Egypt; the house of bondage from which we are redeemed, is a state of spiritual bondage. — Therefore the words, as spoken to us, are to be thus interpreted, "Remember, thou was a servant to sin and Satan, and the Lord thy God delivered thee from this bondage, with a mighty hand and outstretched arm; therefore the Lord thy God commanded thee to keep the Sabbath-day."

As the words in the preface to the ten commandments, about the bringing of the children of Israel out of Egypt, are interpreted in our catechism (and as they have respect to us): [they] must be interpreted [as being] of our spiritual redemption. So, by an exact identity of reason, must these words in Deuteronomy, annexed to the fourth command, be interpreted [as] of the same gospel redemption.

The Jewish Sabbath was kept on the day that the children of Israel came up out of the Red sea. For we are told in Deu. 5:15, that this holy rest of the Sabbath was appointed in commemoration of their coming up out of Egypt. But the day of their going through the Red sea was the day of their coming up out of Egypt. For till then they were in the land of Egypt. The Red sea was the boundary of the land of Egypt. — The Scripture itself tells us that the day on which they sung the song of Moses, was the day of their coming up out of the land of Egypt; Hos. 2:15, "And she shall sing there, as in the days of her youth, as in the day when she came up out of the land of Egypt;" referring plainly to that triumphant song which Moses and the children of Israel sang when they came up out of the Red sea.

The Scripture tells us that God appointed the Jewish Sabbath in commemoration of the deliverance of the children of Israel from their task-masters, the Egyptians, and of their rest from their hard bondage and slavery under them; Deu. 5:14, 15, "That thy man-servant and thy maid-servant may rest as well as thou. And remember that thou wast a servant in the land of Egypt, and that the Lord thy God brought thee out thence, through a mighty hand, and by a stretched-out arm: therefore the Lord thy God commanded thee to keep the sabbath-day." But the day that the children of Israel were delivered from their task-masters and had rest from them, was the day when the children of Israel came up out of the Red Sea. They had no rest from them till then. For though they were before come forth on their journey to go out of the land of Egypt, yet they were pursued by the Egyptians and were exceedingly perplexed and distressed. But on the morning that they came up out of the Red sea, they had complete and final deliverance. Then they had full rest from their taskmasters. Then God said to them, "The Egyptians which ye have seen this day, ye shall see no more for ever;" Exo. 14:13. Then they enjoyed a joyful day of rest, a day of refreshment. Then they sang the song of Moses, and on that day was their Sabbath of rest.

But this coming up of the children of Israel out of the Red sea, was only a type of the resurrection of Christ. That people was the mystical body of Christ, and Moses was a great type of Christ himself. And besides, on that day Christ went before the children of Israel in the pillar of cloud and of fire, as their Savior and Redeemer. On that morning Christ, in this pillar of cloud and fire, rose out of the Red sea, as out of great waters, which was a type of Christ's rising from a state of death and from that great humiliation which he suffered in death. The resurrection of Christ from the dead, is in Scripture represented by his coming up out of deep waters. So it is in Christ's resurrection, as represented by Jonah's coming out of the sea, Mat. 12:40. It is also compared to a deliverance out of deep waters, Psa. 69:1-3, 14, and 15. These things are spoken of Christ, as is evident from this, that many things in this Psalm are in the New Testament expressly applied to Christ. [Compare verse 4 with John 15:25, verse 9 with John 2:17, and verse 2 with Mat. 27:34, 48; Mark 15:23; John 19:29, and verse 2, with Rom. 11:9, 10, and verse 25 with Acts 1:20.] Therefore, as the Jewish Sabbath was appointed on the day on which the pillar of cloud and fire rose out of the Red sea, and on which Moses and the church, the mystical body of Christ, came up out of the same sea, which is a type of the resurrection of Christ — it is a great confirmation that the Christian Sabbath should be kept on the day of the rising of the real body of Christ from the grave, which is the antitype. For surely the Scriptures have taught us that the type should give way to the antitype, and that the shadow should give way to the substance.

Eighth, I argue the same thing from Psa. 118:22-24. There we are taught that the day of Christ's resurrection is to be celebrated with holy joy by the church. "The stone which the builders refused is become the head-stone of the corner. This is the Lord's doing, it is marvellous in our eyes. This is the day which the Lord hath made, we will rejoice and be glad in it." The stone spoken of is Christ: he was refused and rejected by the builders, especially when he was put to death. That making him the head of the corner, which is the Lord's doing and so marvelous in our eyes, is Christ's exaltation, which began with his resurrection. While Christ lay in the grave, he lay as a stone cast away by the builders. But when God raised him from the dead, then he became the head of the corner. Thus it is evident the apostle interprets it, Acts 4:10, 11, "Be it known unto you all, and to all the people of Israel, that by the name of Jesus of Nazareth, whom ye crucified, whom God raised from the dead," etc. — "This is the stone which was set at nought by you builders, which is become the head of the corner." And the day on which this was done, we are here taught, God has made to be the day of the rejoicing of the church.

Ninth, the abolition of the Jewish Sabbath seems to be intimated by this: that Christ, the Lord of the Sabbath, lay buried on that day. Christ, the author of the world, was the author of that work of creation of which the Jewish Sabbath was the memorial. It was he that worked six days and rested the seventh day from all his works, and was refreshed. Yet he was holden in the chains of death on that day. — God, who created the world, now in his second work of creation, did not follow his own example, if I may so speak. He remained imprisoned in the grave on that day and took another day to rest in.

The Sabbath was a day of rejoicing, for it was kept in commemoration of God's glorious and gracious works of creation and the redemption out of Egypt. Therefore we are directed to call the Sabbath a delight. But it is

155

not a proper day for the church, Christ's spouse, to rejoice, when Christ the bridegroom lies buried in the grave, as Christ says, Mat. 9:15, "That the children of the bridechamber cannot mourn, while the bridegroom is with them. But the time will come, when the bridegroom shall be taken from them; then shall they mourn." — While Christ was holden under the chains of death, then the bridegroom was taken from them. Then it was a proper time for the spouse to mourn and not rejoice. But when Christ rose again, then it was a day of joy, because we are begotten again to a living hope, by the resurrection of Jesus Christ from the dead.

Tenth, Christ has evidently, on purpose and design, peculiarly honored the first day of the week, the day on which he rose from the dead, by taking it from time to time to appear to the apostles, and he chose this day to pour out the Holy Ghost on the apostles, which we read of in the second chapter of Acts. For this was on Pentecost, which was on the first day of the week, as you may see by Lev. 23:15-16. And he honored this day by pouring out his Spirit on the apostle John, and giving him his visions, Rev. 1:10, "I was in the Spirit on the Lord's day," etc. — Now doubtless Christ had his meaning in thus distinguishingly honoring this day.

Eleventh, it is evident by the New Testament that this was especially the day of the public worship of the primitive church, by the direction of the apostles. We are told that this was the day that they were wont to come together to break bread. And this they evidently did with the approbation of the apostles, inasmuch as they preached to them on that day, and therefore doubtless they assembled together by the direction of the apostles. Acts 20:7, "And upon the first day of the week, when the disciples came together to break bread, Paul preached unto them." So the Holy Ghost was careful that the public contributions should be on this day, in all the churches, rather than on any other day, as appears by our text.

Twelfth, this first day of the week is in the New Testament called *the Lord's day*; see Rev. 1:10. — Some say, how do we know that this was the first day of the week? Every day is the Lord's day. But it is the design of John to tell us *when* he had those visions. And if by the Lord's day is meant any day, how does that inform us *when* that event took place?

But what is meant by this expression we know, just in the same way as we know what is the meaning of any word in the original of the New Testament, or the meaning of any expression in an ancient language, *viz.* By what we find to be the universal signification of the expression in ancient times. This expression, *the Lord's day,* is found by the ancient use of the whole Christian church, by what appears in all the writings of ancient times, even from the apostles' days, to signify the first day of the week.

And the expression implies in it the holiness of the day. For doubtless the day is called *the Lord's day*, as the sacred supper is called *the Lord's supper*, which is so called, because it is a holy supper — which is so called because it is a *holy* supper, to be celebrated in remembrance of the Lord Christ and of his redemption. So this is a holy day, to be kept in remembrance of the Lord Christ and his redemption.

The first day of the week being in Scripture called the Lord's day, sufficiently makes it out to be the day of the week that is to be kept holy unto God. For God has been pleased to call it by his own name. When anything is called by the name of God in Scripture, this denotes the appropriation of it to God. — Thus God put his name upon his people Israel of old; Num. 6:27, "And they shall put my name upon the children of Israel." They were called by the name of God, as it is said, 2 Chr. 7:14, "If my people which are called by my name," etc. i.e. They were called God's people, or the Lord's people. This denoted that they were a holy peculiar people above all others. Deu. 7:6, "Thou art a holy people unto the Lord;" and so in verse 14, and many other places.

So the city Jerusalem was called by God's name; Jer. 25:29, "Upon the city which is called by my name." Dan. 9:18, 19, "And the city which is called by thy name," etc. This denoted that it was a holy city, a city chosen of God above all other cities for holy uses, as it is often called *the holy city*, as in Neh. 11:1, "To dwell in Jerusalem, the holy city;" and in many other places.

So the temple is said to be a house called by God's name; 1 Kin. 8:43, "This house that is called by name." And often elsewhere. That is, it was called God's house, or the Lord's house. This denoted that it was called a holy place, a house devoted to holy uses, above all others.

So also we find that the first day of the week is called by God's name, being called in Scripture God's day, or *the Lord's day*, which denotes that it is a holy day, a day appropriated to holy uses, above all others in the week.

Thirteenth, the tradition of the church from age to age, though it be no rule, yet may be a great confirmation of the truth in such a case as this is. We find by all accounts that it has been the universal custom of the Christian church, in all ages, even from the age of the apostles, to keep the first day of the week. We read in the writings which remain of the first, second, and third centuries, of the Christians keeping the Lord's day (and so in all succeeding ages), and there are no accounts that contradict them. — This day has all along been kept by Christians, in all countries throughout the world, and by almost all that have borne the name of Christians, of all denominations, however different in their opinions as to other things.

Now, although this be not sufficient of itself without a foundation in Scripture, yet it may be a confirmation of it, because here is really matter of conviction in it to our reason. Reason may greatly confirm truths revealed in the Scriptures. The universality of the custom throughout all Christian countries, in all ages, by what account we have of them, is a good argument that the church had it from the apostles. And it is difficult to conceive how all should come to agree to set up such a custom through the world, of different sects and opinions, and we have no account of any such thing.

Fourteenth, it is no way weakening to these arguments, that there is nothing more plainly said about it in the New Testament, till John wrote his *Revelation,* because there is a sufficient reason to be given for it. In all probability it was purposely avoided by the Holy Spirit, in the first settling of the Christian churches in the world, both among the heathen and among the Jews, but especially for the sake of the Jews, and out of tenderness to the Jewish Christians. For it is evident that Christ and the apostles declared one thing after another to them gradually as they could bear it.

The Jews had a regard for their Sabbath above almost anything in the laws of Moses, and there was that in the Old Testament which tended to uphold them in the observance of this, much more strongly than anything else that was Jewish. God had made so much of it, had so solemnly, frequently, and carefully commanded it, and had often so dreadfully punished the breach of it, that there was more color for their retaining this custom than almost any other.

Therefore Christ dealt very tenderly with them in this point. Other things of this nature we find very gradually revealed. Christ had many things to say, as we are informed, which yet he said not, because they could not as yet bear them, and gave this reason for it: that it was like putting new wine into old bottles. They were so contrary to their old customs, that Christ was gradual in revealing them. He gave here a little and there a little, as they could bear; and it was a long time before he told them plainly the principal doctrines of the kingdom of heaven. — He took the most favorable opportunities to tell them of his sufferings and death, especially when they were full of admiration at some signal miracle, and were confirmed in it, that he was the Messiah.

He told them many things much more plainly after his resurrection than before. But even then, he did not tell them all, but left more to be revealed by the Holy Ghost at Pentecost. They therefore were much more enlightened after that than before. However, as yet he did not reveal all. The abolition of the ceremonial law about meats and drinks was not fully known till after this.

The apostles were in the same manner careful and tender of those to whom they preached and wrote. It was very gradually that they ventured to teach them the cessation of the ceremonial laws of circumcision and abstinence from unclean meats. How tender is the apostle Paul with such as scrupled in, in the fourteenth chapter of Romans! He directs those who had knowledge, to keep it to themselves, for the sake of their weak brethren. Rom 14:22 — But I need say no more to evince this.

However, I will say this, that it is very possible that the apostles themselves at first might not have this change of the day of the Sabbath fully revealed to them. The Holy Ghost, at his descent, revealed much to them, yet after that, they were ignorant of much of gospel-doctrine. Yea, they were so, a great while after they acted the part of apostles in preaching, baptizing, and governing the church. Peter was surprised when he was commanded to eat meats legally unclean, and so were the apostles in general, when Peter was commanded to go to the Gentiles, to preach to them.

Thus tender was Christ of the church while an infant. He did not feed them with strong meat, but was careful to bring in the observance of the Lord's day by degrees, and therefore took all occasions to honor it: by appearing from time to time of choice on that day, by sending down his Spirit on that day in that remarkable manner at Pentecost, by ordering Christians to meet in order to break bread on that day, and by ordering their contributions and other duties of worships to be holden on it — thus introducing the observance of it by degrees. And though as yet the Holy Ghost did not speak very plainly about it, yet God took special care that there should be sufficient evidences of his will, to be found out by the Christian church, when it should be more established and settled, and should have come to the strength of a man.

Thus I leave it with everyone to judge, whether there be not sufficient evidence, that it is the mind and will of God, that the first day of the week should be kept by the Christian church as a Sabbath?

Scripture Index

Genesis

1:5 - 80
1:14 - 81
1:28 - 17
2:2-3 - 18

Exodus

12:2 - 72
16:4-6 - 34
16:22-26 - 87
20 - 16, 34, 62
23:11 - 42
23:16 - 76
31:15 - 100
34:22 - 74
35:3 - 22, 89

Leviticus

19:17 - 84
21:18-20 - 37
23 - 42, 73, 74

Numbers

15:32-36 - 55, 89
28:9-10 92
35:3-5 - 85

Deuteronomy

5 - 62
5:14 - 125
5:15 - 27, 33
6:7 - 19
28:18 - 48
28:25 - 48

Joshua

24:27 - 65

Ruth

1:22 - 75

1 Samuel

14:6 - 66

1 Kings

4:21 - 49
12:27-29 - 49

2 Kings

24:20 - 50

2 Chronicles

36:19-21 - 50

Ezra

2:2 - 51

Nehemiah

10:28-31 - 51, 94
13 - 11, 52, 91, 95

Psalm

20:7 - 66
92 - 134
103:14 - 8

Proverbs

9:10 - 47

Galatians

5:3 - 42

Ephesians

1:13-14 - 106
5:16 - 59
5:22 - 125
5:25-27 - 29, 130

Philippians

1:6 - 30

Colossians

2:14-17 - 42
3:20 - 125

1 Timothy

4:1 - 10

Hebrews

1:3 - 84
8:11 - 105
12:5-7 - 102
13:17 - 122

James

1:27 - 104
4:13 - 93

1 Peter

1:16 - 15
2:22 - 23
4:17 - 47

1 John

2:15 - 130
2:16 - 117
5:3 - 9, 131

Revelation

5:9 - 110
14:13 - 38
21:23 - 109

Subject Index

A

Abib 73, 74
abortion 48
Abraham 49
America, church of 6, 12
American church 126
Amos 79, 80
animals 21, 22
antitype 77
apostate 109
Artaxerxes 52
Assyrians 49
authority 19, 20

B

Babylon 49, 50, 52
Barley Harvest, Feast of 75
behavior 26
Benjamin 49
Bereans 123
betrothal 109
blaspheming 99
Blue Laws 67, 68
bride 105, 108, 109
bridegroom 109
brother 133
business 20

C

calendar, annual 74
calendar, weekly 74
Calvinism 29
Calvin, John 62, 63, 64
captivity, Babylonian 93
car 22
cattle 21

ceremonial law 45
Chapter 11
chasten 48, 57, 102
children 48
Christ
  bride of 2
Chrysostom, Saint 61
church 2
  American 29
  discipline 133
  husband of the 26 *See also* husband
  visible 130
circumcision 92
Confederate Congress 67
Confederate States of America 66
confessions 132
conscience, freedom of 54
County, Bergan 68
courtship 109
Covenant, Old 43
Cox, Robert 63
creation 21, 72
creation order 84
Credobaptist 61
curse 31, 47

D

Daniel 49
David 40, 53
day 79, 80, 82
Day, Preparation *See* Preparation, Day of
defeat 48
desecrate 24
discipline, child 116, 121
disobey 48

INDEX

S

Sabbath
 abrogated 12, 38, 39, 40, 41, 43,
  44, 45, 62, 63
 afternoon 123
 applicability 1
 bonds *See* Sabbath, abrogated
 breaking 5, 11, 39, 41, 48, 50, 52,
  54, 55, 56, 60, 83, 90, 91,
  131, 132, 133
 buying and selling 91, 93, 94, 95
 Christian 43, 61, 78
 command 62, 73, 84, 100
 continuance 44, 45
 day 52, 61, 71, 73, 78
 day's journey 85, 86
 debate 60
 delight 6, 105, 108, 109, 110,
  111, 112, 114, 115, 117, 120,
  126, 133
 doctrine 132
 elimination *See* Sabbath, abrogated
 evening 120
 fulfilled *See also* Sabbath, abrogated
 gift 82, 100
 God, punishing 98
 healing 102, 103, 104
 holy 15, 71, 112
 honor 124
 honoring 41, 111
 ignoring 83
 Jewish 43, 73
 Jubilee 42
 judgment 11, 47
 keeping 2, 5, 9, 11, 12, 37, 61,
  65, 67, 110, 111, 115, 130,
  131
 laws 83
 Lord's Day 44
 mail 67

 mercy 97, 98, 101
 obey *See* keeping
 pollution 36, 37
 practical suggestions 115, 116,
  117, 118, 119, 120, 121,
  122, 124
 punishment 56
 purpose 74
 recreation 64 *See also* Sabbath,
  delight
 rest 12, 52, 83, 93, 99, 116, 119
 sacrifices on 92
 sign 9, 28, 29, 48, 69
 travel on 93
 violate *See* Sabbath. breaking
 weekly 42, 43, 76, 77
 working 40, 100
 year 42, 51, 52
Sabbath, Lord of the 40, 100
sanctification 10, 11, 16, 17, 18,
  19, 24, 25, 27, 31, 40, 48,
  69, 130, 132
Scotland 64
scripture
 inerrancy of 8
 sufficiency of 59
Second London Baptist Confession 62
Second London Baptist Confession
 of Faith 62, 132
servants 20
service 20
seventh day 71
showbread 40
sign 30
sin
 bondage of 7, 27, 34, 42, 77
Sinai, Mount 34
slavery 27, 34, 76
society 23
sodomite marriage 48
Solomon 48
sovereign 25

sports 114
state 23
States, United 67, 68
stranger 37
Superbowl 6
Supper, Lord's 110

T

Tabernacles, Feast of 75
Talmud 85
taskmaster 97
Taylor, Zachary 66
temple 44, 49
testimony 20, 29, 31
Tobiah 52
travel 93
Troas 45
type 72, 77

U

United States 47

V

victorious 48

W

week 79, 99
week, creation 17, 22, 116
week, first day of the 78
weekly calendar 77
Westminster Confession of Faith
  113, 132
wife 1, 2, 108, 129, 130
work 22, 79, 87, 89, 90, 106
work of God 19
world 15, 30
worldview 60
worship 26, 29, 30
worship, family 116
worship service 105

Y

yoke 22, 95

Z

Zedekiah 49, 50